101 KITCHENS

Hydra Publishing
Publisher: Sean Moore
Designer: Gus Yoo
Editor: Sarah Litt

First Published in 2002 by BBC Worldwide Ltd,
Woodlands,
80 Wood Lane, London W12 0TT

Copyright © BBC Worldwide 2002
The moral right of the author has been asserted.

Edited by Alison Willmott

Commissioning Editor: Nicky Copeland
Project Editor: Christopher Tinker and Sarah
Lavelle
Book Design: Claire Wood
Design Manager: Lisa Pettibone
Picture Researcher: Victoria Hall

First American Edition published in 2003
02 03 04 05 10 9 8 7 6 5 4 3 2 1

Published in the United States by
Hydra Publishing
50 Mallard Rise, Irvington,
New York 10533

ISBN 1-59258-007-6

A catalog record for this book is available from
the Library of Congress

Set in Amasis MT, ITC Officina Sans, New
Baskerville
Printed and bound in France by Imprimerie
Pollina s.a. - L88862 c
Color origination by
Kestrel Digital Colour, Chelmsford

BBC Worldwide would like to thank the following
for providing photographs and permission to
reproduce copyright material. While every effort
has been made to trace and acknowledge all
copyright holders, we would like to apologize
should there have been any errors or omissions.

All photographs © *BBC Good Homes magazine*,
with the exception of: Abode 9, 15, 149;
Ariston 63; © *BBC Homes & Antiques* 81, 104,
105, 126, 127, 137, 140, 141, 172, 173; Lu
Jeffery 12, 13; Magnet 37, 75, 89, 101, 111,
117, 121; Plain and Simple Kitchens 45;
Lucinda Symons 78, 79; Wickes 17, 93.

Distributed by St. Martin's Press

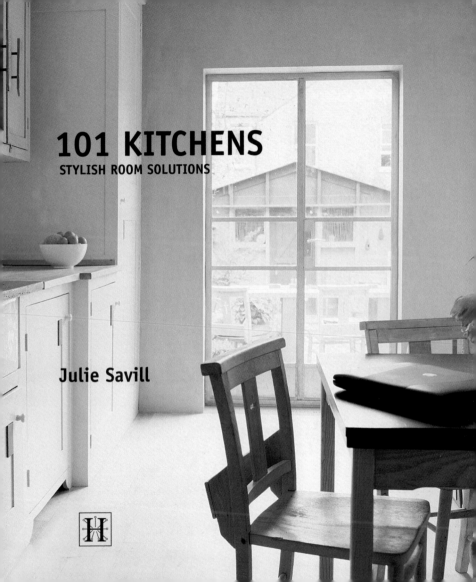

101 KITCHENS

STYLISH ROOM SOLUTIONS

Julie Savill

H

CONTENTS

INTRODUCTION

Imagine moving into a house with a stunning new kitchen, studded with the latest appliances and decked out in just the colors you would have chosen for yourself. Rather dreamy idea, isn't it? Now think about how often that really does happen and you'll realize why having a nicely designed, well turned-out kitchen is the number one asset when you are buying or selling a property. But whether you are on the move or staying put, knocking your kitchen into shape is a good investment, making your home more saleable or seriously improving your quality of life.

The first job in any kitchen makeover is to make a serious and objective assessment of what you already have. If the units are fine but it's the decor that's letting the room down,

you are laughing. With a little inspiration, some paint and maybe a few tiles, you could change the face of your kitchen in a weekend.

Slightly harder work, but still a very cost-effective solution, is the kitchen with sound units that you just don't like the look of. New doors can be bought from specialist companies or made to measure from MDF by a joiner, then simply painted whatever color takes your fancy.

Some kitchens, though, are just beyond redemption and this is the time to put your hands up and admit that a total overhaul is called for. This is where the excitement and possibilities kick in big time. If you are starting from scratch everything is possible – you may decide to relocate the sink under the window or relocate the boiler to free up more space. This is also the time to think about the appliance you want. If you've always fancied a dishwasher but not had the space for it, plan it in now. If a tumble dryer is going to make family life easier, then make sure you give it house room.

Whatever your thoughts, it pays to sketch out a plan of your room and make notes on the things you think you want. Make a few appointments with the free planning services offered by large DIY stores and see what ideas the professionals come up with. At the end of the day you are not obliged to go with any of their plans but they may just have the very idea to overcome your space/light/storage problems.

When it comes down to the style of the units, the shape of the tiles and the color of the walls this book is your design handbook. Among the 101 real kitchens featured here you will get a feel for the type of units you will need to get a particular look and the colors and patterns that you feel you could most happily live with. The rooms are divided into style sections from classic to contemporary but don't limit yourself to the obvious ones that first grab your attention. Styles have natural overlaps and you may just surprise yourself by falling in love with a look you would never have even thought of!

Julie Savill, Editor
BBC Good Homes magazine

The look: Placed at the center of the end wall, the cooker forms the centerpiece of this narrow kitchen, with units framing it on either side. A smart steel and white scheme complements the streamlined layout, while chic design details add interest to the room's minimalist styling.

Color: Ice-white walls and units could make a larger kitchen feel chilly, but work well if you want to freshen up a small room. Stainless steel and other metallic surfaces add to the air of clinical cool, their silvery sheen matching the brightness of the white to create a slick, contemporary look. Jade green countertops provide welcome color without overpowering the room, while the stone flooring and striped rug ground the scheme with natural tones.

Units: The units along the side walls draw the eye to the end of the room, where cupboards and shelves are arranged symmetrically. Narrow open shelving flanking the oven is useful for storing bottles, while a trio of tall wall cupboards on either side of the oven vent reaches to the ceiling. As well as looking stylish, they make efficient use of vertical wall space, providing the same amount of storage as twice as many standard-height units. A step-stool is needed to reach them safely. Other original details include the unusual design of the unit handles and the curved shape of the countertop surrounding the stove.

Counters: If you want to use color in moderation, countertops are generally more discreet than units or walls. Mosaic tiles create a fashionable surface, and their jade green tones with the stainless steel edging give these counters a sleek finishing touch.

KITCHEN TIP
If your layout permits, give yourself generous worktop space on either side of the stove and hob. This allows plenty of room for resting hot dishes safely

The look: This modern kitchen takes state-of-the-art units and sets them within a bright and comfortable environment. Wood surfaces add natural warmth to the room, while areas of open shelving give the furniture a casual, unfitted feel.

Color: The yellow units provide the only color against a backdrop of off-white walls and wooden flooring. The varied tones of the flooring introduce an element of pattern to an otherwise plain scheme. The warm wood tones are repeated throughout the room, on counters, window frames and furniture such as theoven housing, while the white walls ensure a light atmosphere. The yellow has a soft, sophisticated feel, and touches of gold and silver add modern glamour.

Units: The inclusion of open shelves and the way the units are raised off the ground, without kickboards, gives them a trendy, unfitted look. Although the door and drawer fronts are perfectly plain, the 'legs' of the units have curved sides, a stylish, modern design detail. The chunky gold handles also add curvy shape to the room, and their dull sheen complements the pale yellow of the units.

Fridge: If you have a large family, or like to stock up on food in a big way, a fridge-freezer provides impressive storage capacity. They come in a choice of colors, including sleek, reflective stainless steel, which will bring cutting-edge chic to any kitchen.

Accessories: Plain white accessories and tableware with simple shapes complement the room's smart, modern mood, and give a neat look when stacked on the open shelves or arranged along the sill.

KITCHEN TIP
You don't need to pay designer prices to get a quality kitchen, but check the construction is up to par. Drawers should have metal runners, while carcasses should be made from chipboard at least 2cm thick and fully sealed to prevent moisture entering

The look: Kitchen on one side and dinette on the other, this room comprises a casual blend of budget DIY solutions and designer style, combining a stunning steel fridge and modernist dining furniture with MDF units and simple shelving.

Color: White walls and black vinyl flooring set the scene for a plain, modern look, with accents of steel and glass enhancing its contemporary character. The wooden units warm up the look a little, but it's the bright blue countertops and aqua-colored chairs that bring the room to life.

Units: The home-made unit doors, cut from MDF and then varnished, are fitted to existing carcasses, and have metal handles bought cheaply from a local ironmonger. Blue laminate countertops give these basic cabinets a colorful lift. Simple shelving and a metal plate rack take the place of wall units, displaying plain white china and clear glassware which suit the room's minimalist color scheme.

Dining furniture: The dining table and chairs are Italian in origin, and their modernist design creates the perfect mood for informal entertaining. The table has straight, clean lines and a white top that echoes the walls, while the chairs introduce shapely curves and pretty color to soften the overall look of the room.

Windows: The ruched, fine linen blinds also add a softer touch, filtering sunlight without blocking it out altogether. A display of modern vases adds decorative interest on the sills near the dining area.

The look: A light neutral color scheme and pale mellow woods bring a natural but unfussy feel to a tiny kitchen. Metallic details and simple styling set a contemporary mood.

Color: If you want to make the most of limited space, don't crowd out a small kitchen with strong color. Walls painted in white or a light neutral will make the room feel brighter and larger. Here a splashback of pale beige tiles softens the starkness of the white, and tones with the blond wood surfaces. Covering a tiny floor area in wood of a similar shade to the units gives the scheme a more streamlined look than breaking it up with separate blocks of color. The darker tones of the wood-effect worktops add warmth, while flowers and accessories sharpen up the look with flashes of color.

Units: The simple design and metal handles of the units enhance the room's contemporary appeal, and laminate worktops create a practical, easy-clean surface. The glazed door of the tall wall cabinet adds a hint of glamour and allows for the display of attractive china and glassware.

Window: A Venetian blind makes a versatile dressing for a narrow window as it can be adjusted to let in as much or as little light as you want. A metallic finish gives a clean, contemporary look.

Accessories: Too many wall cupboards can make a kitchen feel cramped, but that doesn't mean letting wall space go to waste. Racks hung with utensils, and a wire vegetable basket suspended from the ceiling, are both functional and decorative, helping to add interest to a plain scheme.

KITCHEN TIP
A U-shaped arrangement of units maximizes cupboard and worktop space. However, consider your needs when planning your layout – you might prefer to do without one wall of units in order to fit in a breakfast bar, for example

The look: Classic Shaker-style units get a dramatic and colorful update with smart blue center panels. With its deep shaped alcove, this large kitchen is able to show them off in grand style.

Color: The ultramarine blue of the panels and the light neutral of the maple-effect units are repeated on the walls to create a simple two-color scheme. Big beige tiles cover the splashback, while a toning off-white paint has been used on other walls. The exception is the wall fronting the alcove, which is highlighted in blue to emphasize its attractive curved shape. This provides a link between the units and walls, giving the scheme depth. The varied tones of the wood floorcovering add interest to the large floor area and warmth to the overall look.

Units: Contrasting with the pale maple-effect frames, the dark blue panels give the Shaker-style units a strikingly modern feel. Stainless-steel-effect bar handles and semi-opaque glazed wall cabinets complete the look. If you want units to fit a space exactly, such as this wide alcove, look for a design that includes a selection of different widths. Narrow additions such as the boxy drawers on either side of the oven are useful for filling in awkward gaps.

Lighting: A pendant light hanging low over the table creates an intimate mood for dining. As well as ambient background lighting provided by lamps like these, kitchens should also have plenty of task lighting shining directly onto work areas. Spotlights or slim fluorescent tubes can be concealed on the underside of wall cabinets, and most oven vents are supplied with in-built lighting.

The look: If you hanker after a pared-down minimalist look, remember the less is more principle and clear your worktops of all that clutter! An understated color scheme and sleek, streamlined units also help to set the scene.

Color: To maximize the illusion of space and light in any room, paint the walls in white – a soft off-white is easier to live with than the harsh brilliant variety. Pristine white units underline the clean theme, and ivory mosaic tiles make a subtle splashback. Beech countertops add natural warmth, but the only real color comes from the purple floor tiles. This sophisticated shade smartens up the overall look, and is echoed by the single row of purple tiles that helps to define the pale splashback.

Units: In keeping with the minimalist style, the laminate units have absolutely plain door fronts embellished only with modern metallic handles. The wide doors and white finish of the cabinets give the room an unfussy, streamlined feel. The unvarnished beech-block worktops have been sealed with linseed oil for a low-sheen finish.

Wall shelves: To maintain the room's airy, uncluttered atmosphere, the walls have been left clear of units. Neat open shelving displays carefully selected tableware chosen to fit in with the scheme – white china with clean lines and graphic purple borders.

Floor: A mixture of textures can add interest to a plain scheme, and the floorcovering combines tiles of the same color in two self-patterned designs. Purple tiles with an industrial-style treadplate effect alternate with others that have a rippled texture to form a subtle checkerboard pattern.

KITCHEN TIP
The key to a tidy kitchen is efficient storage. Make the most of cupboard space by fixing racks and shelves inside your units – most kitchen suppliers offer a range of clever interior fittings to help you get organized

The look: With a fresh color scheme that coordinates both kitchen and dining furniture, this room in a tiny flat is designed to be totally functional yet also good-looking enough to put on the style for evening entertaining.

Color: Contemporary shades of aquamarine and lime green harmonize to create a colorful but relaxing look, and a sunny yellow on the walls ensures a cheerful mood. Using a range of different tones adds interest and depth to the scheme: the tiles feature two shades of green, while the blues vary from the pale aqua of the units to the bright turquoise of the tiles and the deeper cobalt-toned paintwork on the table.

Units: Simple Shaker-style units give the kitchen a streamlined look, and white countertops and kickboards keep the atmosphere light and contemporary. Sleek metal handles tone with the cool blue units, while echoing metallic elements such as the stainless steel oven and chrome wall rack.

Dining furniture: The table and chairs have been given the designer look with colorful paint treatments. The pine table has a lime green border on a contrasting blue background: prepare the surface with a suitable primer, then apply two coats of blue satin-finish paint, leaving each to dry. Stick wide masking tape around the outer edge, then add another border of tape inside, leaving a 1.5in gap. Paint the gap with two coats of green paint. When dry, carefully remove tape. Painting chairs in different colors adds a touch of fun.

The look: Industrial metal-framed doors let plenty of natural light stream into this kitchen-dinette. Old church chairs, wooden countertops and a Belfast sink with concrete surround add to the simple, utilitarian look.

Color: A light hand with color enhances the airy feel created by the glass doors. Subtle shades of cool colors – green, aqua and blue – create a harmonious combination that makes the kitchen a relaxing spot for family meals. The pale flooring reflects light from the doors, while the wooden countertops and furniture add warmth with natural color and texture.

Units: The home-made wooden units have Shaker-style panels and are painted in duck-egg blue. They show an interesting attention to detail, with tiny rectangles of painted wood decorating the corner of some panels, plus unusual handles made from terracotta plant markers on the wall cupboards.

To copy this idea, attach the flat head of two screws to the back of a plant marker using epoxy resin, then thread a nut and washer onto each screw, leaving plenty of space between the door and handle. Fix to the door by threading another nut and washer onto the screw behind the door.

Sink: An arched alcove makes a natural space for the Belfast sink. Its surround was made by pouring mixed concrete into a wooden box, with letters cut from foam to create the jokey 'Everything but'. The plate rack is made from timber and aluminum poles.

The look: Galley kitchens can easily look cramped and cluttered, but this one has become an aisle of style, with contemporary colors and fittings freshening it up and streamlined storage solutions creating room to breathe.

Color: Lime green makes a refreshing wall shade for the south-facing room, and complements the light, modern coloring of the birch units. Metallic fittings and appliances add a steelier edge to the scheme, while blue and white in bold geometric patterns – the striped Roman blind and checkerboard flooring – sharpen up the look.

Units: The birch units have the simplicity and elegance of Shaker-style furniture, albeit in a contemporary design. Fitting them with a matching beech countertop, and concealing the dishwasher behind a semi-integrated door front, has given the run of units a streamlined look. Neat round door knobs echo the many other metallic elements in the room.

Splashbacks: Aluminum splashbacks have high-tech chic, are easy to wipe clean and also reflect light, helping to keep the atmosphere bright and airy. A mosaic covering creates a more decorative effect behind therange, with a subtle scattering of blue tiles amid a plain white background.

Wall racks: Leaving walls clear of cupboards gives a small kitchen a more spacious look. Wall-mounted racks are less obtrusive, and an adaptable modern system holds anything from cooking utensils to wine bottles. These smart aluminum rails can be hung with different fittings. A discreet rail fitted across the top of the splash-back allows racks to be added at any point along it and moved with ease.

KITCHEN TIP

In a galley kitchen, the sink and hob should be on the same side of the room so that you aren't forced to cross from one side to the other carrying heavy pans

The look: A combination of different materials adds interest to an understated color scheme in this small modern kitchen. Natural tones and textures give the room an inviting feel, while the glimmer of brushed metal adds a smart café air.

Color: From the pale wood of the units to the stony effects of worktops and flooring to the metallic finishes of appliances and accessories, the mix of materials creates a subtle interplay of textures. Walls washed with chalky white emulsion, and splashback tiles in an equally pale shade, create a plain, minimalist backdrop. Only the floor breaks out of the palette of light neutrals, with dark slate-effect tiles shot through with flashes of warm amber to ground the scheme.

Units: The pale oak wood cabinets are topped with granite-effect work surfaces and have hammered metal knobs in a brassy color. The simple Shaker-style panelling of the doors enhances the natural but contemporary appeal of the blond wood.

Appliances: Contrasting with the natural tones of the furniture, the metallic surfaces of the appliances add a slick, contemporary edge to the scheme. The microwave and oven have a matte, silvery finish, while white appliances feature trims in brushed metal, touches of which are repeated around the room to unify the look.

Window: A neat Roman blind in a soft woven linen provides a minimal, light-friendly window treatment. Fitting it above the recess means that it can be raised and lowered without sweeping the line-up of plants from the windowsill.

The look: This tiny kitchen makes up for in glamour what it lacks in size. Leaf and bamboo-design wallpapers cover both walls and units to create a unique and streamlined look with an oriental flavor.

Color: Subtle patterns in soft jade on a cream background give the wallpapers their sophisticated style, and create a calming atmosphere. Silvery floorboards tone with the greens, while adding a luxurious sheen. The laminate countertop introduces a deeper shade of jade to strengthen and enrich the look.

Units: The kitchen is so small that the MDF units had to be made to fit. Covering units with paper is an unusual move; in this small apartment a coating of varnish affords enough protection, but a paper covering may not withstand the knocks suffered by the average family kitchen. Twiggy door handles reflect the bamboo design of the paper and the silvery color of the floor.

Floor: Silver-painted floorboards reflect light and increase the feeling of space. To prepare boards for painting, hammer down any protruding nails. If you have bare, sanded boards, apply knotting over the knots and wood primer over the whole floor. When dry, rub with fine wet-and-dry paper, and wipe using a cloth dampened with white spirit. Fill gaps with wood filler. If your boards are varnished, stained or already painted, simply sand and wash with warm soapy water before painting. Protect the paintwork by applying two coats of clear floor varnish.

Accessories: Even the smallest kitchen has space for a few decorative accessories. The mirror with paper-covered frame and the colored glass fish ornaments add to the individual character of the look.

The look: Flexibility is a must in the modern kitchen and, with a little ingenuity, even a tiny one can double as a dining room. Movable storage and foldaway furniture are your keys to a magical transformation.

Color: Cool, contemporary aqua creates an upbeat mood for both cooking and casual dining. The chairs add a deeper blue to vary the tone, while dark brown flooring and red accents warm up the look. The two tabletops get their color from a covering of Formica – one in plain red, one in bold stripes.

Furniture: Open shelving provides storage without crowding the room, and freestanding furniture can easily be moved to change the mood. Lightweight wheeled racks can be brought center-stage for cooking and then pushed aside when it's time to eat. You could also add fabric covers to conceal their contents. A table with two tops works twice as hard – these are made from different-sized pieces of MDF covered with Formica, and each can be rested on metal trestles to make a table or work surface. When not in use they stand on a shelf above the countertop. Chairs that can stack or hang on the wall are another space-saving solution.

Window: A tall, narrow window needs a neat, light-friendly dressing. A Venetian blind can let in plenty of light but also does a thorough job of shading strong sunshine with the slats fully closed. A wooden design gives an informal, natural look.

The look: The colors of fresh ripe fruit promote a feeling of vitality, so try zesty citrus shades to invigorate and energize. Bold blocks and circles against a crisp white background give this fun look plenty of impact.

Color: A cocktail of red, orange and yellow will go down well if you're looking for a stimulating color scheme, but don't go overboard – primary colors work best on a backdrop of white, so paint areas of color on a white wall or use white tiles to break up colored ones. Try not to be too regimental or symmetrical – uneven shapes and patterns will give you a kick-start on bleary-eyed mornings. Add further color accents in furniture, tableware and even with bright appliances.

Furniture: If you plan a colorful look, keep units plain and simple in style to avoid too fussy an effect. The flat-fronted white base cabinets have a countertop to match, plus sleek, streamlined handles. The wall units add weight to the color theme, with a covering of red Formica. The dining furniture is also unfussy yet fun, the curvy shapes of the table and chairs echoing the circles painted on the wall behind.

Splashback: The mosaic tiling highlights the attractive shelf feature of the splashback wall by using different background colors above and below. Mosaic tiles are easiest to apply when bought in sheet form – to create a pattern, glue your sheet of background tiles in place, then carefully cut through the backing paper using a craft knife to remove individual tiles. Replace them right away with ones of a different color, then leave until the glue is dry.

The look: The future's bright for kitchens – units are going beyond the pale, and you'll find a myriad of brilliant work surfaces for a truly high-energy atmosphere. It's hard to believe that this furniture is straight from shops – the result is pure designer.

Color: Sharply contrasting blues and oranges jostle together for a look that is lively and uplifting. The key to using two vibrant hues like this is to ensure that one dominates – in this case orange leads the way. Pace and pattern come from the bold retro-style circles on the splashback tiles, while accessories and appliances in blue and orange take the color theme all the way. Touches of white freshen the look, and the pale wood flooring provides a calming base to balance the bright colors.

Units: Plain design reinforces the impact of the colorful units, while the clear plastic handles add a funky finishing touch. In kitchens where the walls play second fiddle to the units, using the second color on the countertop and kickboards as well makes for a punchier contrast. Here they bring the blue into closer conjunction with the orange cabinets.

Splashback: Tiles with a retro circle pattern are interspersed with plain white ones, their uneven arrangement creating an offbeat look that fits in with the room's fun feel. These tiles were bought ready-patterned, but you could copy the look by cutting a circular stencil from stencil card or acetate, then using it to paint white tiles. Apply a tile primer first to enable the colored paint to adhere to the smooth surface.

The look: Colored door panels give a contemporary twist to this simple and traditional unit design. Polished stone and beech veneer surfaces add refined natural appeal to create a look that brings together character, color and comfort.

Color: Because they boast the only real color in the room, the blue panels catch the eye. Otherwise, wood dominates the scheme, used for the splashback as well as the units to set the tone for a warm, inviting atmosphere. The light beech makes the mood contemporary rather than country, and plain white walls keep the room feeling fresh and airy. The flooring grounds the scheme with a darker color, while stainless steel fittings brighten the surrounding wood with reflected light.

Units: The beech veneer units have blue laminate panelling and D-shaped nickel handles. A variety of different cabinets makes for a lively look; the blue panels are instantly noticeable as a design feature, but small 'finger pull' spice drawers, a built-in wine rack and deep drawers with textured glass fronts also add interest to the line-up of units, as well as versatile storage options. Polished granite makes for a luxurious countertop and provides a smart contrast with the wood tones.

Floor: Ceramic or stone-tiled floors are hard underfoot but extremely durable. These dark tiles set off the light units beautifully, and look fantastic when polished to a mirror-like finish. However, if you have children running around your kitchen you'll prefer a less slippery surface.

Accessories: Generous wall shelving provides space for a country-style display of wooden bowls and colorful ingredients in glass jars. Glitzy stainless steel accessories add a touch of modern glamour along the worktops.

KITCHEN TIP
Take advantage of the computer-aided design facilities offered by many kitchen retailers. Using the measurements of your room, they can produce a 3-D image to show you how it would look if fitted with their units

The look: Proper planning lets you cram lots into even the smallest kitchen. Carts on wheels, tables that fold flat and wall-mounted storage are the quick tricks you need to know.

Color: Cool green has a space-enhancing effect on a small kitchen, especially when used to cover the entire wall surface. This fresh but muted tone is easy on the eye and complements the wood-effect vinyl flooring and birch veneer units. The stainless steel oven vent and other metallic fittings add a slick modern edge to the scheme.

Furniture: The units come from a range that can be bought as either freestanding or built-in furniture, with legs or plinths sold separately. Carts on wheels can easily be moved around, which is particularly handy if they have a work surface on top. Any kitchen with a little spare wall space can accommodate a dining area. All you need is a wall-mounted table which folds down when no longer needed. A foldaway bar stool can be hung out of the way on the wall.

Cooking: Why have an oven if you never use one? Keep it simple with a hob set into the work surface, then use the space underneath to store a cart filled with pans. If you do want an oven and range, you might find that a combination microwave can handle most of your cooking demands.

Wall racks: If you're short of cupboards, put walls to work by fitting racks for cooking essentials. They are great for keeping spices and oils close to hand, and make it easy to find utensils without rummaging around in drawers.

The look: Let medical chic provide the cure for your outdated kitchen. Cool tonal colors and sharp lines team up with chrome, glass and rubber for the ultimate in clean living.

Color: Ice-white units set the tone for this clinical look, and their dazzling brightness is offset by the blues and greys on the walls. The muted shades of these toning colors relax the effect while keeping a cool atmosphere, and blend with the grey metallics of the appliances and fittings which add all-important sparkle and shine. Pale blue floor tiles with a glittery effect add an unexpected touch of fantasy.

Furniture: Plain white units fit this look perfectly – team them with chrome handles for high-tech cool. Forget kickboards, and leave legs on display to mimic free-standing style. A table with a wipe-clean top can double as a work surface – make it from MDF at a fraction of the price it would cost to buy. Paint the MDF with varnish or gloss paint, and leave to dry. Cut rubber or vinyl flooring to fit, spread the table-top with strong adhesive and stick in place. Set on trestle legs.

Splashbacks: Sheets of glass make practical industrial-style splashbacks; ask a glazier to cut them to size. Use safety glass for clear good looks, or Georgian wire for a simple grid effect. If your wall is uneven, laminated glass will hide the lumps.

Accessories: The noticeboard is made of paper sandwiched between Lucite sheets which are held together with long chrome mirror screws and mounted away from the wall using chrome piping. Write on it with wipe-off marker pen. White plastic baskets, clear glassware and stainless steel pans complete the feel-good style prescription.

The look: With wall-to-wall units and worktops all in beech, warm wood tones have the upper hand in this room, but glossy handmade Mexican tiles and cool gleaming metals also vie for attention.

Color: The mellow wood of the units is thrown into relief by the deep colors of the walls and splashback. The verdant grassy shade on the walls tones with the rich blues and greens of the tiles to create a strong but relaxing background. The long, unbroken lines of units ensure that wood tones predominate, but the blond color of the beech keeps the look light and modern.

Furniture: Clean lines and Shaker-inspired panelling give the beech units contemporary style. The original handles were discarded in favor of curved metal designs which echo the shine of the steel oven. For a coordinated effect, choose dining furniture that reflects the style of your units; this modern set is in matching beech.

Splashback: Handmade tiles are expensive, but their irregular shaping and coloring give them a more individual, less monotonous appearance than a wallful of machine-made ones. As they are all slightly different shapes and sizes, you may prefer to ask an expert to lay them. This splashback has sand-colored grout, which looks softer than the usual stark white and tones with the wood of the units.

Oven: The steel oven, extractor and splashback introduce a touch of high-tech chic, and brighten the room by reflecting light. Metal splashbacks are easier to clean than tiles, so offer more efficient protection for the area behind a hob. Some oven suppliers sell ready-cut splashbacks, or you can get one cut to size by a metal merchant.

The look: Bring your kitchen right up to date with the industrial gleam of stainless steel. Used to front the units and cover the splashback, it stamps cutting-edge style on this room, even when surrounded by timeless natural wood and warm terracotta paintwork.

Color: The wooden flooring and maple veneer wall cupboards and worktops balance the cool glimmer of the steel cabinets with natural tones, creating an interesting contrast of textures. The terracotta-colored walls also add a touch of rustic warmth, offsetting the sleek steel to ensure that the large room feels cosy rather than clinical. Using the same color scheme and flooring in the dining area provides continuity, linking the two rooms and making the most of the long view from the kitchen, while sharply contrasting white woodwork highlights the wide doorway between them.

Units: As well as the steel finish, it is the wide flat fronts, clean lines and long metal handles of the base units that give them their ultra-modern character. Drawers of varying depths provide versatile storage beneath the large hob for utensils and pans. The wall cupboards have the same simple design as the base units but provide textural contrast with maple veneer, a light, contemporary wood finish that complements the stainless steel beautifully. The worktop and kickboards are made from solid maple.

Lighting: Good lighting is essential in a kitchen. Large lights fitted beneath the central wall cupboard provide efficient illumination over the hob, while smaller spotlights further along cast their rays onto the rest of the worktop. Stainless steel has valuable reflective properties, and the splashback and accessories boost the power of artificial light by bouncing it into the room.

KITCHEN TIP
Clean smears from stainless steel using a damp cloth and mild detergent. To keep it shining, buff with a soft cloth and a little baby oil or olive oil

The look: In a kitchen just 8ft wide, it's quite a challenge to find space for an eating area as well as plenty of storage. This sleek scheme pulls it off, and provides a touch of retro style into the bargain.

Color: The combination of yellow and dark brown creates the retro feel. The units are painted in 1950s yellow, offset by dark brown cork tiles on the floor. Dazzling white walls help to open up the room, while metallic fittings and glass accessories also reflect light.

Units: Fitted units make the best use of space in a small kitchen, but you can create an old-fashioned, unfitted appearance by alternating units with appliances. These cabinets consist of inexpensive carcasses fitted with made-to-measure doors. A stainless steel strip glued around the worktops adds a stylish finishing touch. Space-saving shelves are a clever substitute for wall cupboards.

Breakfast bar: Clearing units from one wall has created space for an eating area. To make a narrow table, a leftover piece of countertop has been turned into a breakfast bar. Fixed to the wall on one side, it is supported by legs cut from chrome tubing.

Splashback: The white, beige and brown mosaic splashback epitomizes the 1950s look. To create a pattern, first work out your design on graph paper. Buy mosaic tiles in sheet form, and glue the white tiles in place, then mark on their paper backing where each colored tile needs to go. Using a scalpel, cut around these squares and insert colored ones, positioning them to maintain the correct width of grout gap.

KITCHEN TIP
If space is tight, remember that you need to allow at least 4ft in front of appliances and units to allow the doors to open safely

The look: Trendy kitchen designs can date quickly, but good old wood has timeless appeal. These maple-effect units combine the warm and natural feel of wood with unfussy modern styling for an easy-to-live-with contemporary look.

Color: Light woods have a more modern appearance than darker or orange-toned grains such as oak and pine. The beech laminate flooring adds further natural tones to the scheme, and beige splashback tiles keep the overall look calmingly neutral. The dark worktops and appliances give the scheme a smarter edge, while accents of bright blue and lime green liven it up with splashes of color.

Units: The maple-effect units provide the look of real wood at a more affordable price. Chamfered edges add stylish detail to the plain doors, and the long metal handles reinforce their modern character. Glass shelves are a light, unobtrusive touch in the open-fronted display cabinet, and the metallic appearance of the worktops also has contemporary cool.

Appliances: Stainless steel appliances are the top choice for many modern kitchens, but if you have kids you may be put off by the thought of all those sticky fingermarks. This stove and fridge-freezer look as smart as steel, but are in fact made from toughened plastic, which is easier to keep clean.

Splashback: Traditional brick-shaped tiles work just as well in a contemporary setting and can give a more individual look than the more common square ones. A band of blue tiles running around the base of the splashback echoes the colors of the toaster and stool seat.

The look: Blocks of vivid color and straight, angular lines make an impact across three rooms in this bold modern scheme. In an open-plan setting, different colors can be used to define separate living areas.

Color: If you want to use a selection of bold hues on surfaces near to one another, stick to harmonious colors – that is, three or four from the same side of the color wheel. The starting point for this color-rich kitchen was the vivid green of the units. The bright blue and purple walls are of equal tonal strength, while the look gets a fresher lift from the white floor tiles and the pale green paint used on the splashback.

Layout: Open-plan kitchen and dining rooms are popular because they allow cooks to talk to dinner guests while preparing meals. However, you may not want guests to enjoy a full view of your kitchen operations, and continuing the units part of the way across the opening creates a barrier.

Units: The units get their bold color from a coat or two of paint. Before decorating wooden units, sand them down to provide a key. On melamine, apply a suitable primer to give a base for the colored paint. Glass inserts in the wall units offer visual relief from the panels of strong color, while simple metal handles echo the silvery worktops and stainless steel sink. The kickboards are picked out in the same pale green as the splashback.

Accessories: Tableware and vases in blue and green keep the color theme going. Accessories with simple shapes look at home amid the clean, modern lines of the room.

KITCHEN TIP
If possible, choose paints formulated for use in steamy rooms. Major paint manufacturers offer special kitchen and bathroom ranges designed to resist moisture, grease and grime

The look: A radical redesign has turned a previously cramped kitchen and tiny dining area into one bright and inviting living space. A smart and functional scheme in glittering steel and white puts the icing on the cake.

Structural work: To open up the two rooms, the dividing wall was removed and an RSJ (reinforced steel joist) installed to support the load. The back door was replaced with a glass-panelled one, to flood the room with light. Always consult a builder if you are thinking about removing walls, or you could end up knocking down more than you bargained for! Major alterations like these are a job for professionals.

Color: The new sense of space is enhanced by snow-white walls and stainless steel surfaces which bounce light around the room. Pale wood flooring unites the dining and kitchen areas, and a narrow splashback of cream mosaic tiles runs around the walls. Just a few splashes of brilliant color are enough to lift this neutral scheme, the hot pinks and purples forming a stunning contrast with the clean white walls.

Furniture: As part of the redesign, a walk-in pantry was created under the stairs, so there was no need for endless built-in cupboards. Instead, stainless steel worktops have space beneath for a vegetable cart and bin, and matching steel-clad doors are fitted where needed. The high-tech glamour continues with a stainless steel oven and chic metal-framed dining furniture.

Soft furnishings: Made from silk dupion, the table runner and curtains add luxury as well as color to the room. The roller blind at the window is made from an equally colorful Indian cotton.

KITCHEN TIP
If you have an understairs cupboard near the kitchen, clear out the junk, fit it with shelves and turn it into a pantry. Make shelving shallow so that items can't get hidden and forgotten, and store heavier foodstuffs on lower shelves

The look: A combination of modern metallics and natural wood gives this kitchen a laid-back contemporary look. An eye-catching radiator adds a stylish touch, and a shot of brilliant pink from the dining room next door really livens things up.

Color: Pale lemon yellow and cool aqua (used on the radiator wall) make a refreshing backdrop for the mix of wood tones and shimmering metallics. The beech flooring, salvaged from a school gym, has been stripped of dark varnish to lighten the mood, and now complements the beech units and pine door. Using contrasting colors in neighboring rooms creates an interesting effect when doors are left open: hot pink draws the eye through into the more vibrantly decorated dining room.

Units: The beech units are sufficiently simply styled to sit comfortably in a contemporary scheme, but their deep panels and wooden handles add a relaxed country air. Black countertops smarten them up, and the stainless steel oven and splashback provide a steely contrast for their warm wood tones.

Wall racks: The metal racks above the worktop are both smart and functional. As well as offering shelf space on top to keep pans within easy reach of the cooker, they can be hung with any number of hooks to provide storage for utensils. The wine rack makes use of dead space behind the door.

Radiator: Although standard models don't contribute much to the style of a room, radiators with designer looks or unusual shapes can make eye-catching features. This tall design takes up a minimal amount of horizontal wall area, leaving more space free for units or other furniture.

The look: Designer-style units and top-notch appliances ensure sleek style. However, you don't have to pay designer rates for good-looking furniture – these units are from a competitively priced range by a retail chain.

Color: Whatever the price of your units, the colors you choose can go a long way towards making a style statement. Mint green has a cool, sophisticated aura, especially when teamed with plenty of slick metallics. Beech-effect details warm up the look a little with subtle natural tone and texture, while checkerboard PVC flooring in mottled grey and white adds a slightly quirky feel.

Units: The pale peppermint color of the units is distinctly individual, as are smart designer details such as the tiny curved metal handles and the reeded glass panels on the wall cupboards. These contemporary materials combine comfortably with the beech-effect countertops, kickboards and shelves. The symmetrical arrangement of the wall units makes a focal point of the stylish oven vent, with curved display shelves flanking it on either side to draw the eye in and add to the visual interest.

Splashback: The splashback has a metallic appearance but is in fact covered with a laminate product made to look like brushed aluminum. Used on the whole of the wall, it adds a luxurious light-enhancing sheen to brighten the room and complement the stainless steel fittings and accessories.

Oven vent: If you do a reasonable amount of cooking, good extraction is essential to keep the air clear. This handsome oven vent has a curved glass canopy which gives it a less imposing and more slimline look than all-steel, chimney-style models.

KITCHEN TIP
If you want a fully fitted kitchen, ask two or three retailers to plan for you, then compare prices and designs. Draw up your own plan first by sketching a layout to scale on graph paper so that you form a clear idea of the features you want to include

The look: Color is the simplest way to update the atmosphere of a room or emphasize detailing. Here ice blue warmed up with cherry red evokes a retro feel in a contemporary setting.

Color: In any blind poll, blue comes out top – it's a universally popular color and never seems to date. Warmed up with reds and pinks, blue springs to life, and when combined with cherry red it is evocative of the 'atomic' colors popular in the 1950s. Vinyl floor tiles laid in a checkerboard design add pattern with pace, while metallics lend the look an industrial feel. Steel runs through this kitchen as a theme, emphasizing the coolness of the blue and reflecting light around the room.

Units: The unit drawers are made from beech, and the brown in the wood works well with the blue and red to soften the look. Metal handles form a high-tech contrast with its rich, natural color. The kickboards and worktop are made from MDF, and covered with blue Formica, that favorite 1950s material.

Splashback: Aluminum treadplate has a distinctly industrial look, and is the perfect choice if you want to make a feature of metallics. Available from metal merchants, it serves as a durable splashback – fix it to the wall with strong adhesive or, if the surface of the wall is uneven, use screws with mirror fittings. It can also be used to cover floors.

Accessories: The blue, red and steel scheme is carried through to the cookware, crockery and other accessories. Like the metallics, glassware possesses valuable light-reflective qualities that can help to make a small kitchen feel bigger and brighter.

KITCHEN TIP
White goods no longer live up to their name, and colorful fridges or ovens can make eye-catching features. Smaller appliances are also available in a range of zingy shades

The look: The odd traditional element such as a butler's sink can add a touch of old-fashioned country charm to a modern kitchen. Simply styled units and a bright color scheme put the emphasis on contemporary looks.

Color: Buttery yellow units combine with pale cream walls to create a cheerful but relaxing atmosphere. The splashback tiles add zingier color, with a lively mix of blues and contrasting citrus shades. Their orange and yellow are repeated in the window blind, while the smart canisters on the countertop echo the lighter shade of blue. The natural tones of the stone flooring and wooden worktops blend well with the units.

Units: Shaker-style units give a neat contemporary look, and the long metal handles are distinctly modern. However, the painted finish and beech countertops hint at a more traditional country style.

Hiding appliances behind unit doors makes for a streamlined effect – the dishwasher is semi-integrated, which means that the controls have been left uncovered.

Sink: Butler's sinks originate in country farmhouses but are becoming a popular choice for any style of kitchen. Wide and deep, they make it easy to wash big pots, and also prevent water from splashing out when used with a high-necked tap. A monobloc mixer tap is the favorite design for modern kitchens as water temperature can be controlled through one outlet – this design is traditionally styled, with a high, curved spout and traditional-style controls.

Window: The Roman blind adds definition and color to the wide window. The patterned fabric is edged with a narrow border of plain orange to give it a more finished look.

The look: Glass surfaces and white walls throw light around to make the atmosphere clean and bright in this neat, modern kitchen-diner. At the same time, wooden units and flooring keep the mood relaxed and easy-going.

Color: In a scheme strong on contemporary simplicity, white walls create a pristine foil for wood surfaces. They also enhance the airy atmosphere by reflecting natural light. Glass and steel furnishings do the same, making up for the lack of color by adding a glamorous shimmer to the room. In a plain neutral-colored scheme, natural textures add interest – the variation in the flooring's tone and grain introduces an element of pattern.

Units: Wooden units used in a contemporary setting add natural warmth to the room, adding up to a look that's cool but comfortable. The Shaker-style panelling of these doors works well with the modern decor, while softening the overall effect with a hint of traditional style. Chunky metal handles echo the stainless steel oven vent and accessories.

Appliances: Having your oven built in at eye level means no more bending down to lift out heavy dishes. A microwave is fitted above this single oven, and both have sleek doors made from opaque glass. Positioned near the window, their light-reflective properties really shine. The extractor above the hob is equally streamlined, with straight lines and spare design.

Dining furniture: With their large surface areas, long tables often form the focal point of a kitchen, so choose a style that suits your scheme. This glass-topped design sets the tone for the air of contemporary chic, which is continued by the shapely white plastic chairs.

The look: Create your own designer-style kitchen by modifying plain units. These cupboards are fitted with homemade MDF doors, but chic details dress them up to give a distinctly different look. High-quality appliances and an elegant window blind also add an upmarket air.

Color: A neutral scheme of clotted cream, grey and soft white has classic impact that softens a modern design. The white walls provide a fresh, light-enhancing backdrop that highlights the richness of the cream-colored paint used on the units. Aluminum appliances and fittings add a high-tech glimmer to reinforce the room's modern appeal, while grey slate floor tiles offset the pale neutrals with a darker contrast.

Units: It's easy to make new doors for existing units – just get 2cm MDF cut to size, and use your old doors as a template to mark positions for hinges. These DIY doors have been embellished with narrow strips of MDF, glued in place before painting. Smart handles also help to give a professional finish – square ring-pull designs in brushed steel are echoed by the sleek steel edging that gives a lift to the white laminate worktop.

Appliances: If you've made over your units for pocket money, your budget might run to the latest in modern appliances. This oven and extractor have a soft aluminum finish, which is more fingerprint resistant than its stainless steel sister. The splashback is made from aluminum sheeting.

Window: Patterned with a sophisticated floral design, a Roman blind made from fine linen adds further designer style while allowing lots of light to filter through. Keeping a blind partially lowered can help to improve the proportions of a tall, narrow window.

The look: Warm tones of orange add a sociable, positive energy to a kitchen. What's more, it's a color that's said to aid digestion! Brighter citrus-style shades may be too startling of a morning, but a lighter, softer orange will ease you more gently into the day.

Color: For maximum effect, use the orange on both the walls and units, and keep the warm tones coming with natural wooden flooring and furniture. Cream-colored tiles cool down the look a little, adding a band of light relief between the two blocks of strong orange. The wide range stove and its vent also brighten the overall effect with the reflective shimmer of stainless steel.

Units: The unit doors, which are fitted onto existing carcasses, come from a company that supplies made-to-measure MDF doors ready to paint, and have been decorated in the same shade as the walls. Their simple Shaker-style panelling works well with the soothing modern-country mood of this room, and the wooden worktops echo the natural flooring and furniture. Leaving the walls free of cupboards allows the colorful paintwork to make its full impact. Instead, orange-painted shelves create a casual display of foodstuffs and tableware, keeping them within easy reach.

Dining furniture: A chunky oak table with trestle-style base reinforces the cosy country feel. The wooden frames of the director's chairs add further natural texture, but their informal style keeps the overall look contemporary.

Splashback: The tiles have a textured, handmade look that gives them a subtler, softer appearance than flat ones. Their rich cream coloring provides a light but gentle contrast to offset the bright orange.

The look: Traditionally styled wooden units get a fresh update with a coat of cream paint and a set of chic, contemporary handles. With new beech countertops thrown in, the result is a look that's light and bright but also easy to live with.

Color: Soft cream complements the classic deep-panelled design of the units but also creates a light atmosphere that suits a small contemporary kitchen. Plain white splashback tiles continue the brightening effect and also enhance the richness of the cream by providing a clean contrast. Beech counters add a touch of warmth, with glowing natural color and texture.

Units: The wooden units were stripped back before painting but a quicker method is to apply a multi-surface primer, designed to provide a key for paint on even a smooth, varnished surface. Chrome handles that shine as brightly as the stainless steel appliances add a modern finishing touch. Leaving one wall cabinet without a door puts favorite china on show and makes it more accessible. End shelves also provide a display forum to round off the rows of cabinets, their tiny fences adding decorative detail.

Countertop: Although existing units can be updated with paint, it's not so easy to revamp old countertops. However, for all but DIY novices, it's simple enough to replace them, so it's worth completing your makeover with beautiful new ones. Wood is pricier than plastic laminate but it has a natural charm, and solid beech counters provide a hard, practical surface. Wood does require care to maintain its looks, though – beech should be rubbed with oil every few months to prevent it drying out.

The look: In textural terms, this room combines old and new, teaming oak units with metallic flooring and design details. The walls brighten things up with a blast of color, creating a modern, livable look for a kitchen in an old house.

Color: Cornflower-blue walls add depth, contrasting with both the pale wood of the units and the steely metal surfaces. The dolly-mixture assortment of tiles covering the splashback combines deep and pale blues, which echo the walls and fridge, with bright orange and yellow, all arranged at random for a lively effect.

Units: The oak units combine modern design and steel handles with a timeless feel. For variety, some of the wall units have checkerboard-patterned glazed doors while others are fronted by clever roll-up metal blinds. Along with the stainless steel kickplates and metal dining furniture, these reinforce the slightly industrial feel of the room. To add shape to the run of base units, the oven workstation and cabinets extend out into the room, giving the impression of a curved line.

Floor: The flooring resembles industrial-style metal treadplate but is actually a PVC lookalike, sold as tiles, which is just as hard-wearing but much warmer underfoot.

Lighting: While a pendant light with a chrome shade provides general background lighting, the counter is more efficiently lit by bright halogen spotlights fixed into the underside of the wall unit and into the top of the alcove above the oven..

KITCHEN TIP
Avoid using fabric or paper light shades in a kitchen as they are likely to harbor grease and cooking odors. Glass and metal fittings are more practical

The look: This kitchen takes a step back to the 1930s, its design and decor reflecting the age of the house it occupies. It's a mixed bag of old, new and recycled, with original floorboards, salvaged counters and contemporary units customized to fit the look.

Color: Subtle retro shades of primrose yellow and pale sage green create a calming atmosphere, and complement the mellow shades of the wooden flooring. White splashback tiles freshen the look, and stainless steel details add a contemporary glint, while the dark wood of the countertops contrasts with the lighter colors, adding depth to the scheme and striking a more traditional note.

Units: To recreate old-fashioned looks, avoid a streamlined layout and break up runs of units by interspersing them with appliances or freestanding furniture. Simple flat-fronted modern units adapt well to 1930s style when painted in the right color and fitted with curvy metal handles. Panels of tongue-and-groove boarding fitted to cover the sides of the end units also give a nostalgic feel. The countertops are made from old science lab desks which came, along with the Belfast sink and taps, from a clearance at a local school. Remnants have been used to make the wall shelves.

Splashback: A white-tiled splashback can seem plain and clinical, but brick-shaped tiles give a more individual look than the normal square ones, and their utilitarian character suits the mood of this room.

Floor: This 1930s house still has its original floorboards. They were already in good condition, but regular polishing has enhanced their glowing natural color and attractive knotty texture.

The look: After the ornate furniture and dark colors of the Victorian era, the Edwardians brought a lighter, more elegant look to interior design. These cream units reflect that airy feel, combining it with classic details to create a convincing modern take on a period-style kitchen.

Color: Deep red forms a rich contrast for cool cream, making the light units really stand out against the bold backdrop of the wall color. Painted in a cream chosen to match the units, architectural details such as the coving and window frame are also highlighted. The granite countertops and solid oak flooring, both polished to a luxurious shine, add warm natural color and texture to the scheme.

Units: Features such as turned pilasters and raised center panels give the units their classic charm, and the multi-paned glazed fronts of the wall cabinets are particularly evocative of Edwardian elegance. Intricacies such as beading on door and drawer frames add to the effect, and hammered cast-iron knobs with a dimpled effect make a stylish finishing touch. Open shelves at the end of the island unit provide attractive display space for books and old-fashioned accessories.

Countertops: Granite is an expensive choice for a counter, but it has natural beauty and a timeless appeal. It is also hardwearing and provides a cool surface useful for making pastry. The least porous of the stone surfaces, it is practically stainproof and easy to clean, although it can be damaged by alcohol. If you can't afford the real thing, you'll find plenty of granite-effect designs in man-made products such as laminates.

The look: For an understated modern-country feel, choose panelled units in white or cream rather than a natural wood finish. In this long galley kitchen, they give a smart, streamlined look, with lines of vivid splashback tiles injecting a shot of welcome color.

Color: Clean and bright, white or cream will give even the most traditionally styled units a refreshing modern look. If cupboards cover most of the walls, the splashback tiles may offer almost the only chance to add lively color, and they do it very effectively here. Arranged in stripes running all along the wall, the rows of brilliant tiles peep out from between the units to make a dramatic feature of the kitchen's length. Flooring can also help to warm up the room; rustic terracotta-effect tiles soften the look with natural color.

Units: These units are from an affordable range by a DIY store and were bought wholesale price with a 45 per cent discount – so if you plan a major refit it's worth waiting for the sales. With Shaker-influenced styling, the units offer a balance between simplicity and tradition, with subtle panelling to enliven their plain finish and nickel-effect strap handles adding classic detail. Concealing appliances behind unit doors increases the streamlined effect; you can simply box them in, have them fully integrated or leave just the control panels uncovered for ease of operation.

Cart: Keeping vegetables in open carts or baskets is a good idea as it means air can circulate around them. A wheeled cart is a handy addition to any kitchen, providing fully mobile storage.

The look: Ornate metal accessories and curved panels on unit doors bring a feeling of old-fashioned romance to this individually styled room. Freestanding furniture adapted for kitchen use adds to the casual but decorative effect.

Color: A restrained scheme of creams and dark browns creates a restful, traditional atmosphere. Cream walls keep the overall look light, contrasting with the dark wood counters and floorboards. Cream and brown also come together on the units, while a narrow tiled splashback blends with the walls. A few flashes of bright blue, on the window frame and range table, give the sober scheme a lift.

Units: The units have doors custom-made to match the freestanding cupboard in the corner. Both units and cupboard are painted, with the panels in brown to highlight their curvy shapes, and the rest in cream to match the walls. Pretty metal door knobs enhance the

traditional look of the furniture.

Freestanding furniture: The unfitted pieces add character but are also practical: the tall cupboard has generous storage capacity, a neat cabinet houses the oven and microwave, and a blue table supports the range. Screwed to the wall, the table has had its back legs cut off. It is decorated with a distressed paint effect, while tiles in toning colors protect the wall behind.

Accessories: The cage-like orb hanging on a chain from the ceiling is a ship's lantern. Together with a large painting in dark tones, this quirky accessory reinforces the room's air of romance.

KITCHEN TIP
Unconventional sources can turn up original furnishings. Old pews, desks and shop fittings adapt well to kitchen use, so keep an eye open for clearances at local stores, churches and schools

The look: Custom-made units give an individual look, and some companies allow you to mix and match styles within one room. This kitchen combines a range of finishes to create a classic country-house feel, with striped walls and an imposing oven canopy adding an air of grandeur.

Color: Traditional shades of dark green and cream are in tune with the style of the units, and counters and flooring with rich wood tones also enhance their classic country character. The earthy shades of the wide wall stripes tone with the natural colors and textures in the room. Painted first in undiluted cream and terracotta, they have been washed over with a darker terracotta to give a cloudy effect.

Units: Choosing different materials and finishes for each block of units creates an unfitted appearance. The custom-made cupboards also feature different traditional designs, the green block with many smaller panels and drawers, and the cream cupboards with broader panelling. The concave corner cupboard helps to soften the square look of the kitchen. The painted units have a distressed finish, which gives the room a comfortably lived-in feel.

Oven canopy: A striking feature of the room is the impressive chimney-style canopy, which frames the stove and conceals the extractor hood. Built from wood by the company that supplied the units, it has been painted to resemble stone.

Pot rack: The wooden hanging rack above the sink is made from an old Indian shutter suspended by chains from the ceiling. Its dark wood suits the traditional style of the kitchen, and its fretwork design can cope with plenty of hooks for displaying pots and utensils.

The look: Black is an unusual choice of color for units but it gives a smart, sophisticated look, especially when teamed with an icy blue on the walls and flashes of stainless steel in fittings and accessories.

Color: Black can be difficult to live with as it absorbs all color energies and puts none back into the room, so you may want to avoid it if you use your kitchen for relaxing as well as cooking. It's best used in a large, light-filled room, and balanced with lighter and warmer colors. Although the far wall is covered with black cupboards, the nearer one is free of wall units to allow for a large area of refreshing pale blue. Warmth comes from the wooden flooring and counters.

Wall border: A border of squares adds an eye-catching detail, and introduces black near ceiling level to balance the look further. To copy this design, cut a square out of a piece of stencil paper, and fix the stencil to the wall to paint white squares. When dry, stick four strips of masking tape onto each square, carefully lining them up with the outer edges. Paint the smaller square inside black. Repeat when dry, to paint tiny grey squares inside the black ones.

Units: Double-panelled doors and dark wood counters have a traditional feel, but metal handles echo the high-tech shimmer of the stainless steel accessories. Glass-fronted wall cabinets help to break up the dense effect of the black units. A set of steps may be useful for helping you to reach high cupboards – but might also tempt small children to scale the counters!

The look: A creative attitude to color can give a kitchen an individual look. Pink walls perk up a roomful of oak units and dark tones for a look that feels warm and cosy but definitely not 'olde worlde.'

Color: With dark slate flooring, grey stone-effect countertops and splashback tiles featuring a medley of greens, this room has elements of a classic country look. However, marshmallow pink walls are an original addition, bringing a blush of color to the scheme. Somber forest greens offset their sugary quality, while the pale wood of the units also provides a calming antidote.

Units: Oak has always been a traditional favorite for cabinets, and these units combine its warmth and sturdiness with light, modern coloring and unfussy design. Made from solid blond oak, they feature up-to-date details such as stainless steel handles and glass door panels etched with a checkerboard design. Units in a range of different sizes make the most of the space in this kitchen, and the clever shelf built around the oven vent mobilizes a normally redundant area to store and display cook books and pans.

Wall racks: Getting utensils and crockery off the counters and onto the walls is nothing new but, while more traditional rooms favor wooden plate racks or peg rails, these sleek stainless steel rails have a neater, trendier look. Packs of hooks are sold separately, allowing you to fit as many items as you can along one rail.

The look: White walls team up with wood surfaces to create a clean but comfortable environment for this light-filled kitchen. The room has been enlarged by an extension at the far end, providing space for a dining area.

Color: White is a fantastic brightener if you want to make the most of light and space. Here it covers the walls and ceiling, paintwork blending seamlessly with splashback tiles. Its starkness is softened by the abundance of natural tones and textures, from the rustic floorboards and tiles to the more refined wood of the units. The tablecloth contributes the only splash of color, its country-style checks bringing a homely feel to the dining area.

Furniture: The Shaker-style units have metal handles in classic designs and countertops in a pale-colored laminate. The dining table is an antique store buy, while the chairs were found in the trash. If you spot something you like in the trash or on the street, ask the owners if you can take it. In legal terms, removing it without permission amounts to theft.

Windows: Extending the kitchen offered the chance to brighten it with extra windows. The one above the sink provides a garden view and has been matched as closely as possible to the existing sash window. The skylight in the sloping ceiling is a more effective source of light as sun streams straight in, without trees to check its progress.

Floor: The change in flooring indicates where the extension begins. As the original boards would have been difficult to match exactly, the owners have gone instead for a contrasting effect with quarry tiles.

The look: Crisp white units, light wood surfaces and bright, uplifting color give this kitchen its refreshing modern-country charm. Inspired by traditional Italian design, the elegant units add an air of subtle romance.

Color: Green walls complement the country-fresh feel of the room and provide a bold foil for the dazzling white units. Using a punchy rather than muted green ensures a bright, modern mood, and choosing countertops made from pale wood also gives the country look a light update.

Units: The units give classic style a contemporary twist, combining traditional details such as raised panels and multi-paned glass doors with a slick high-gloss finish and simple white knobs. A combination of wide and narrow cabinets creates an unusual asymmetric effect. Another notable feature is the peninsular wall unit, useful for increasing storage if you're short of wall surface. With glass doors on both sides, it also makes a great display cabinet. It is secured to the wall at one end, and supported at the other by a single strut fixed into the counter. Most of the counters are made from blond beech, and the splashback is covered with matching wood.

Breakfast bar: A length of counter jutting out from one side of the island unit creates a long breakfast bar. Fixed at the right height for chairs or stools to slide underneath, it continues around the end of the unit to form a stylish modern feature.

Accessories: Colorful pottery and glassware in the display cabinets reflects the kitchen's classic Italian inspiration, while stainless steel accessories bring out the more contemporary side of its character.

The look: Before you start planning a kitchen, think carefully about how you want to use it, especially if space is limited. In this room designed for a keen cook, a professional-style oven came top of the priority list, even though it's a little on the large side for a kitchen measuring just 10 x 6.5ft.

Color: Although light colors boost the feeling of space in a small room, you may prefer the warmth and character that stronger tones can offer. If you want an intense wall shade, a cool hue such as blue will have a less cramping effect than fiery red or orange, and painting the ceiling white will prevent the color from overpowering the room. For a streamlined look, keep the scheme simple, with bold blocks of color covering large areas rather than several shades used in small amounts. Here the blue walls form a rich contrast with the orange tones of the wooden units and the quarry-tiled floor.

Units: Richly colored woods such as pine, cherry and oak give a kitchen a warm, inviting feel. These cabinets have a simple design, with frame and panel doors and plain drawer fronts, but metal cup handles strike a more traditional note. Their silvery sheen echoes the stainless steel of the oven and blends with the grey countertops.

Oven: Professional or commercial-style range cookers have up to eight burners, plus large ovens, so are ideal if you like entertaining or have a big family. An efficient vent is essential over an oven this size; this range is teamed with a matching stainless steel model, and more shining steel covers the splashback.

The look: If elaborate pilasters and panels are a little too 'olde worlde' for your taste, but Shaker styling seems rather too plain, then look out for units that combine clean lines with modern decorative detail. This design offers the natural beauty of wood in a light, contemporary color.

Color: Blond woods allow you to use timber units throughout your room without making it feel like a country farmhouse. They have a subtler charm than the more knotty, colorful grains of oak or pine, and their light tones sit well with modern interiors. The pearwood color of these units is complemented by a wooden floorcovering in similar tones to create a totally natural environment. To avoid stealing attention from the units, the walls are painted in plain, understated off-white. Black granite-effect counter-tops provide a smart contrast for the lighter colors.

Units: The units are made from solid lime, finished to a delicate pearwood color, and their contemporary design is characterized by straight lines and geometric detailing. The door fronts feature simple recessed panels, but a few are also decorated with a cutout pattern of four small squares. Along with the grille design of the glass-fronted wall cabinets, these help to add visual interest to the overall effect. Curved metal handles complete the contemporary styling.

Accessories: A fisherman's lamp, wire baskets and accessories in natural materials inject a hint of rural style to complement the wood surfaces and wicker storage hampers. On the wall above theoven, stones and shells are displayed in wooden boxes to make simple, natural pictures.

KITCHEN TIP
An island unit with surfaces on two levels makes food preparation easier by offering a choice of working heights for different tasks

The look: Recreate the sun-drenched atmosphere of a French farmhouse with rustic wooden furniture and a vibrant color scheme lifted straight from the fields of Provence.

Color: Lavender blue and corn yellow arecomplementary colors; they sit opposite each other on the color wheel so are guaranteed to create a successful and enriching contrast. The yellow was chosen to match the existing counter tiles, and forms a warm foil for the mixture of natural woods in the room. The newly laid splashback tiles bring the blue and yellow together in big, bold squares.

Units: The pine frames of the existing units and wall racks fit in perfectly with this country look, so have been left unpainted. The cupboard doors, previously a dull shade, have been reinvented with a coat of bright blue paint. Some are fitted with 'crafted' handles in a beaten metal finish, while others have recessed matte metal door pulls. The mixture of natural wood and painted surfaces gives the units a casual, uncoordinated look, and traditional open wall racks provide ample display space for zingy Mediterranean-style pottery that matches the room's colors.

Dining furniture: A rough-grained wooden table and a set of old-fashioned chairs are must-haves for a cosy farmhouse-style kitchen, and will soon turn it into the heart of the home.

Splashback: The colorful splashback tiles are laid over old ones, saving the messy job of chipping them off the wall. A double layer of tiles will stand out from the wall, but you could add thicker beaded or pencil tiles along the top edge to conceal this.

KITCHEN TIP

Good preparation is essential when painting units, especially older ones. Make sure they are clean, using sugar soap to get rid of stubborn grease. Sand back wooden units or apply a suitable primer before painting with a gloss or eggshell finish

SHAKER

The look: Deep red creates a dramatic backdrop for natural textures in a room that focuses on the country charm of the Shaker look. Wood, whether painted or natural, covers every surface, and woven accessories increase the rustic rating.

Color: Deep red points straight towards New England style. This rich shade forms a warm foil for the pale beech counter-tops and peg rail, while toning with the darker wood of the floorboards and the deep natural browns of the wicker and sisal baskets. The cream used to paint the wood-panelled walls lightens the scheme and prevents the dark colors from becoming too oppressive.

Walls: The walls are covered with tongue-and-groove boards which give a panelled, country-house look. They are also ideal for concealing surfaces that are in less-than-perfect condition. Available as unfinished wooden planks from DIY stores, they slot together easily and can be painted in the color of your choice once fitted to the wall.

Units: The base units have the classic Shaker-style design, with a rectangular recessed panel surrounded by a wide, flat frame. The old-fashioned metal pull handles are not strictly Shaker but add to the country charm. Mini chests of drawers mounted above the peg rail make unusual wall units. Painted to match the base cabinets, they have knobs made from short lengths of dowel screwed end on to each drawer.

Accessories: A wooden peg rail is an instantly recognizable feature of Shaker style, providing simple but good-looking wall storage. Natural woven accessories also reinforce the look; wicker baskets slide neatly into open units, while sisal containers can serve both as plant pots and utensil holders.

KITCHEN TIP
To protect wood-panelled walls from damp, apply a coat of clear matte varnish after painting

The look: A kitchen with space for a slim table and a couple of chairs will become the most used room in the house. Mix painted furniture with plain wood, and turn tea towels into instant curtains for easy-going family style.

Color: The buttery yellow used on the walls, the grey paintwork on the chairs and the cream finish on the units are all colors associated with Shaker style, and their soft tones team well with the natural wood of the table. Blue mosaic splashback tiles and accents of red brighten things up, while the smart black counters and chrome accessories add a hint of urban cool to this relaxed country look.

Units: Painted units with tongue-and-groove-style panels and simple metal handles have a nostalgically rural feel, and make a perfect complement for the butler's sink and range oven. The countertops are made from Welsh slate for sleek but natural good looks.

Splashback: Fashionable mosaic tiling helps to give the room a contemporary edge. Mosaic tiles can be bought attached to backing sheets, which makes it easy to apply them to large areas. Glue the sheets in place with tile adhesive then, when dry, peel off the backing paper and grout as for normal tiles.

Window: The tea-towel curtain emphasizes the laid-back character of the look. Hung café-style, over just the lower half of the window, it provides privacy without blocking out much light. Tea towels make excellent no-sew curtains – simply punch eyelet holes along the top and thread them onto a wire. You can buy eyelet kits, complete with hole punch, from craft, art and fabric stores.

SHAKER

The look: Earthy tones, natural textures and gleaming copper cookware keep country traditions alive in this room, while the spare Shaker styling and pale wood of the units lend the look a fresher, more contemporary feel.

Color: A deep shade of terracotta covers the walls and beamed ceiling, forming a rich foil for the blond woods of the units and flooring. The cream-painted cupboard brightens an otherwise gloomy corner, joining with the cream tiles above the oven to freshen the room's overall look.

Units: These solid birch units are perfect for a country kitchen but also simple enough to work with more modern styles of decor. The island unit plays up the rustic theme with a beech work surface and wicker baskets, while sleek granite counters give the other units a more contemporary feel. The tall cupboard makes efficient use of corner space to provide generous storage capacity. It also helps to add visual interest, providing a break among the blocks of units to suggest the appearance of a traditional unfitted kitchen.

Racks and rails: In a cottage kitchen, hanging racks are as decorative as they are useful. The overhead rack not only shows off handsome pots and pans, but also draws the eye towards the attractive beamed ceiling. A peg rail is a hallmark of Shaker style, and serves as a display vehicle for smaller accessories and tools.

Accessories: Old-fashioned copper cookware adds an authentic touch to a country setting and complements the warm tones of wood and terracotta. Bring the outdoors inside with leafy plants in rustic terracotta pots and bunches of herbs hanging from rails.

KITCHEN TIP
If your kitchen is too small for an island unit, a butcher's block on wheels is a handy alternative. It gives you extra work surface and storage facilities and can be pushed to one side when you need to reclaim your floor space

The look: A cool blue and cream color scheme, classic Shaker-style units and light, natural wood tones form a chic but relaxing backdrop for semi-formal entertaining in this elegant kitchen-dinette.

Color: A muted shade of Shaker-inspired blue teams up with contrasting cream to create a calming environment. With the natural wood tones of the countertops and table to warm it up, the simple two-tone scheme needs little additional color. The cream is used on both the walls and wood-panelled splashback to provide a uniform backdrop. Highlighting the window frame in blue, and leaving the window undressed, makes a feature of its attractively deep recess.

Furniture: The blue-grey color of the units is in character with their Shaker styling, and the simple wooden door knobs are also in line with the look. A wall cabinet with clear glass panels makes it easy to find cooking ingredients at a glance. Smooth polished woods bring a refined air to natural style; the beech counter is echoed by the smart wooden dining table.

Sink: A white ceramic sink has classic traditional looks and goes well with the wooden countertop. This is a practical modern style designed to sit in the counter, with an integral draining board. A tall faucet that can be swivelled aside helps to avoid chipping crockery as it is lifted out of the sink.

Tableware: Plain tableware in white or pastel colors looks cool and contemporary – try a pale blue to reflect the color of the units. Mix it with wooden bowls, practical cutlery and chunky tinted glassware for easy-going style.

KITCHEN TIP
Positioning the sink beneath a window gives a cheery outlook to anyone on washing-up duty

The look: The Shakers believed that a kitchen should look calm, cool and efficient. This room recreates American country style using classic Shaker colors – strong but plain – and folksy accessories made from natural materials.

Color: Blue-grey and brick red, played off against each other in a subtle contrast, add character to a set of flatpack units, while cream walls provide the perfect tranquil backdrop. Authentic Shaker colors are available from specialist paint makers, but close equivalents could be found among mix-to-order collections in DIY stores. Grey stone-effect countertops and limestone flooring tone with the deep colors to complete the harmonious effect.

Units: Although the panelling on the units is more elaborate than typical Shaker-style borders, they pass muster when painted in the right colors. To keep the look calm and understated, limit the red-painted panels to a few selected units. Using red on details such as the kickboards and the borders of the glazed wall cabinets carries the contrast throughout the room without overdoing it.

Accessories: Turn on New England charm with heart motifs and natural textures – woven samplers and napkins, rustic baskets and wooden bowls all capture the spirit of the style created by the early settlers. If you want to show off tableware and containers, choose pieces with clean lines and plain colors, such as the cream-colored china and functional food canisters on display behind the glass doors of the wall cabinet.

The look: Home-made doors fitted onto existing carcasses have given this room a budget transformation – Shaker-style doors are particularly easy to make as their design is so simple. Painting them in different colors adds an individual look.

Color: Greyed-off shades of green and blue spring from the traditional Shaker color palette, but using them on different doors and drawers shows an innovative approach to the style. Combining them with plenty of cream keeps the overall look light, while the beech countertop and oak flooring fill the room with the natural warmth of wood grain.

Units: There's no need to rip out old units if you want a new kitchen – just replace the doors. To make Shaker-style doors, ask a timber merchant to cut pieces of 2cm-thick MDF to size. Fit each one with

hinges, then cut lengths of 2.5 x 5cm timber to form a frame on the front. Glue the timber to the MDF with strong contact adhesive, fill any gaps to create a smooth surface, then prime and paint.

Floor: In a room that leads into the garden, the dark, knotty finish of the solid oak flooring helps to disguise any dirt brought in. If you can't afford solid wood flooring, take a look at veneered planks, which have a thin covering of wood laid over a core of chipboard or similar material.

Accessories: Utilitarian accessories are in tune with Shaker design principles. The tin container and canisters combine functionality with style by echoing the deeper blues used on the units. Shelves and racks on the wall keep the worktop clear of clutter.

KITCHEN TIP
If you want to fit new doors to existing carcasses but don't have the DIY skills to make your own, find a company that sells ready-made doors without the units – see the where to buy list in this book or try your phone book for local suppliers

SHAKER

The look: If you yearn for the comfort of a country kitchen but don't want to compromise your modernist standards, check out 21st-century rural style that makes the most of the appeal and texture of wood. This kitchen is totally freestanding – it'll cost you, but you can take it with you when you move.

Color: Let the wood surfaces grab all the limelight by choosing an understated neutral for your walls. This mushroom shade looks warmer than white or cream, yet is light enough not to overpower the units. Add just a dash of color, with accents of leafy green in plants and tableware, plus a stripy rug to liven up a plain floor.

Units: Unfussy Shaker styling and metal handles give these solid beech units a modern-country look. Freestanding kitchen furniture is expensive, but you needn't buy everything at once – just add pieces when you want. This design includes wall cupboards to match the freestanding base consoles. To vary the look, some are glass-fronted, while base units without doors can be fitted with wicker baskets to emphasize the country style.

Sink: Fitting a freestanding kitchen is easy – all you need to do is get a plumber to plumb in your sink. Console units can be bought with sinks included; this white ceramic design looks good with wood, while the straight single-lever tap enhances the contemporary style of the room.

Accessories: Rural and modern styles have been mixed and matched: a traditional plate rack sits alongside plainly styled units, and rustic wooden cookware contrasts with steely metallic flowerpots. Plain white china combines clean modern lines with unpretentious country appeal.

The look: Walls colorwashed in dusky pink add a hint of townhouse elegance to cream-painted Shaker-style units, while wood and stone-effect surfaces keep this look grounded in rural tradition.

Color: Cream is a versatile color for units as it can be teamed with a wide range of wall shades. Rich or muted tones such as this pink will give a room a traditional feel, but you could change the mood by substituting lilac, lime green or orange to create a modern look.

Walls: Applying paint as a colorwash breaks up the solid effect of strong shades to give a softer appearance. Start with a base coat of undiluted emulsion in a lighter shade, and leave to dry. Add water to the darker color until you get the strength of wash you want, then apply to the wall in crisscross strokes using a wide brush.

Units: Birch knobs and honey-toned wooden work surfaces complement the soft cream paintwork of the cabinets. A combination of countertop finishes adds visual interest; the stone-effect surface on the island unit provides a smart contrast with the wood. Glass-panelled wall cupboards enhance the room's elegant feel by displaying fine china. They also draw the eye up towards the unusual semicircular window.

Oven alcove: The contemporary stainless steel oven gets a more traditional look by being built into an old fireplace alcove in the style of a range cooker. Units fill in the spaces on either side, and a combined peg rail and shelf keeps utensils and ingredients handy. The pediment across the top adds a classic-style finishing touch and a mantelshelf for displaying decorative accessories.

The look: Arranging units in a U-shape divides this kitchen into two distinct areas – for cooking and dining. Coordinating their colors and materials gives the large room a unified look.

Color: Fresh blues and aquas combined with off-white walls create a light, contemporary look, while glowing timber adds natural warmth to ensure a homey atmosphere. The honey-toned counter is echoed by the wooden dining table, while the chairs continue the scheme into the dining area with a turquoise paint finish and seat covers featuring the same stripe as the blind.

Furniture: Flatpack units sold without doors form the base of the kitchen. The doors and wall shelving are homemade from MDF and painted in two shades of blue. The wooden chairs have been revamped with paint and new seat covers. Drop-in seats are easy to re-upholster: remove the seat, center it on a square of fabric and staple one side of the fabric to the base. Pull the fabric taut on the opposite side, and staple in place. Repeat for the remaining sides, forming neat tucks at the corners.

Splashbacks: A narrow band of marble-effect mosaic tiles runs above the units, their neutral shades complementing the natural texture of the worktop. A sheet of glass protects the wall behind the range, and helps to brighten the room by reflecting light from the window.

Floor: Reclaimed floorboards mellow the scheme with the comforting look of old wood. Search for them at junk yards, along with other materials gleaned from old houses – but make sure that the wood is in good condition before you buy.

The look: If you like the simplicity of Shaker style but want to give it a slightly more sophisticated twist, try deep red. This darker shade from the Shaker palette gives a smarter look than its more popular pastels. Shiny chrome accessories and smart handmade tiles make their mark among these maroon-painted units.

Color: Deep maroon is a strong color to choose for a small kitchen, but in this room the plain white walls and ceiling manage to maintain a feeling of space by reflecting natural light from the window. A row of neutral-colored splashback tiles softens the contrast between the white and maroon, and tones with the beech-block countertops.

Units: Painted units with simple recessed panels and wooden knobs have classic Shaker looks. These have been made by a carpenter to fit around the sink and appliances, which usually works out cheaper than buying a custom-made design from a kitchen company. Built from MDF and fitted in place by the carpenter, they have been painted by the owners.

Sink: Butler's or Belfast sinks are great if you want traditional country character, but they aren't the most practical choice if you don't have a dishwasher. They tend to be very deep, and long periods of washing-up can lead to backache – now there's a good excuse!

Splashback: Handmade tiles with distinctive designs add an individual touch to a kitchen. They don't come cheap, so you might face a choice between quality and quantity, but a single row of designer tiles can look just as effective as a whole wall covered in standard ones.

KITCHEN TIP
As well as allowing you to choose any color you want, painting your own units means it's easy to change the look of your kitchen. All it takes is simple repainting rather than a complete refit

The look: Soft Shaker blue looks light and contemporary but also strikes a chord within a country setting. Here rustic floorboards, natural textures and copper details offset its cool character to create a look of perfect harmony.

Color: The blue is used on most of the woodwork in the room. Teaming it with a gentle cream keeps the look relaxing but refreshing, while pale wooden counters help to balance the darker floorboards. The white-painted door adds a brighter touch, especially when it catches the light streaming in from outdoors.

Units: The pure and simple design of Shaker-style units lends itself particularly well to a painted finish. Pale birch work surfaces and plinths complement the cool, contemporary nature of the blue, while antique-effect copper handles give the units a more traditional edge. An island unit makes use of the large central floor area – reminiscent of the large farmhouse table that is a traditional feature of country kitchens, it goes one better by providing storage features as well as extra work area, including an attractive built-in wine rack.

Splashback: A wooden splashback is fine above work surfaces, but tiles offer more effective protection for the wall behind the range cooker. Plain white tiles can look boring, but laying them diagonally adds an extra dimension.

Accessories: Painted pottery, terracotta cookware and baskets made from wire and wicker are all country-style essentials. Wooden trugs and crates used as vegetable holders add further natural texture and rustic cred.

The look: Thanks to their clean lines, Shaker-inspired units work well in contemporary settings. This large family kitchen combines them with bold color and industrial stainless steel for a striking but laid-back modern look.

Color: While pale blue enhances the quiet simplicity of the units, walls in a tangy deep-toned orange turn up the heat to give the high-ceilinged room a warmer, more friendly feel. Pale maple countertops bridge the gap between the two contrasting colors, and provide a natural contrast for steel surfaces such as the oven and vent. The ceiling and woodwork are painted in soft white to keep the room looking fresh, as bright colors soak up natural light.

Furniture: Leaving the walls free of cupboards gives a more open look, and allows the orange to make a real impact. To add interest to the plain table, it has been decorated with a wide border, applied using pale blue eggshell, which matches the ready-painted units. Metal garden chairs provide casual seating.

Window: The boldly striped blind smartens up the scheme with graphic pattern and emphasizes the height of the room. Roman blinds are easy to make if you buy a kit from craft stores which provides all the necessary fittings and instructions.

Noticeboard: A magnetic noticeboard takes care of paperwork – from shopping lists to postcards. This one was made by sticking sheets of tin plate onto hardboard using PVA glue. Strips of wooden beading cover the sharp edges.

The look: Reflecting the fashion for 1950s looks, this contemporary kitchen design features key styling elements from that decade: units with gently rounded edges, bold tiled flooring and light, bright finishes in wood, glass and stainless steel.

Color: The fresh shades of aqua and cream used for the units are as popular today as they were in the 1950s. Combining them with wooden detailing and a rich yellow on the walls adds warmth to the overall look. Bold black and white checkerboard flooring joins with shiny stainless steel appliances to inject a smart city feel.

Units: Clean lines and soft curves were important features of 1950s design, and chamfered doors and drawers give the essential rounded edges. A new trend was set with the inclusion of materials such as wood and glass in interior design, which is reflected here by the use of pearwood-effect casing and ribbed glass insert panels for some of the units. Chunky steel-effect handles complete the retro look. On the central unit, the stone-effect laminate counter doubles as an eating area, extending beyond the units to allow space underneath for diner-style bar stools.

Appliances: A large fridge-freezer emphasizes the air of urban chic, its vast reflective surface helping to brighten the entire room. More high-shine stainless steel features in the oven vent and the splashback above the range.

Accessories: A 1950s-style radio and small appliances in bright colors boost the room's retro credentials. A hanging rack attached to the splashback keeps cooking utensils handy for the range.

The look: This scheme was inspired by the dresser at the far end of the room, which is a copy of an original 1950s design. A fresh color scheme of blue and cream, along with plenty of chrome details, strikes the right style note, but the overall effect is calming rather than kitsch.

Color: Light blue and cream create a fresh, airy atmosphere in this large kitchen, with yellow accents adding a touch more energy. Plain cream walls make a balanced backdrop for the blue-painted dresser and units, and the two colors come into closer contact on the floor, where they form a checkerboard pattern. Steel and chrome appliances and accessories complement the coolness of the blues.

Units: The dresser has been made to order, in the style of a 1950s original. Tall units like this make maximum use of vertical wall space by providing generous storage capacity and, if freestanding, can go with you when you move house. The base units, also made to order, mimic the smooth-edged cupboard doors of the dresser and are topped with a practical laminate work surface. Steel handles add the finishing touch to the doors and drawers.

Splashback: Blue-tinted heat-resistant glass makes a sheer, light-reflective splashback that's easy to keep clean. Try your local glass merchant for sheets of colored glass, and ask whether they can cut it to size for you.

Floor: The checkerboard floorcovering consists of blue and cream tiles made from rubber, which is softer underfoot than linoleum and also kinder to any crockery that might tumble onto it.

KITCHEN TIP
If you're lucky, you can still pick up original 1950s furniture in good condition from antique shops. Spruce up wooden pieces with a fresh coat of paint and smart new handles for the latest style must-have

The look: Shiny chrome accessories and refreshing shades of blue and green continue the retro 1950s feel of this apartment into the kitchen, but are cool enough not to overpower the small, narrow space. Flat, unfussy unit doors give a streamlined look.

Color: If you want to fill your kitchen with color while still enhancing the illusion of space, use shades from the cool side of the spectrum. Light blues and greens create a bright, airy feel, especially when teamed with the blond wood tones of the counters and laminate flooring. The fresh pistachio used on the walls and the ice-blue paintwork on the units give a subtle suggestion of 1950s style, while the splashback tiles embolden the look with a band of brilliant greens and turquoise.

Units: The units are the result of DIY ingenuity and design flair, a budget alternative to designer styles. The carcasses are cheap ones bought from a DIY store, but their original doors have been replaced with plainer, made-to-measure MDF designs. These have been painted and fitted with curved chrome handles.

Wall: The hole in the wall not only adds an interesting feature, with its unusual egg shape echoing the curves of the red stool, but also serves a practical purpose by letting more light into the enclosed part of the narrow kitchen.

Accessories: Chrome pots and pans really help to brighten the small space by bouncing light around, while comple-menting the fittings and accessories in the desk area. Attention to detail gives any scheme a finished, unified look – the plug socket is also in matching chrome.

The look: Inheriting a kitchen with original 1950s units inspired retro style for this room. Bold checkerboard flooring and shiny metallic appliances keep the cabinets company, while prettily patterned curtains and tiles give the look a country twist.

Color: The warm cream on the walls complements the color of the units, while black and white vinyl tiles arranged in a checkerboard design create classic retro-look flooring. The handmade fruit-design tiles on the splashback add to the air of 1950s frivolity, their neutral background blending in with the walls. The rose-patterned curtain fabric, which picks up on the cream and red of the units, softens the overall look, while the wooden chairs and checked tablecloth bring a homey feel to family dining.

Units: These colorful, curvaceous metal units with Formica countertops were the must-have kitchen furniture of the 1950s. Originals like these in good condition are now difficult to find, but persistence pays off. This kitchen already had the base units in place, and matching wall cupboards were eventually tracked down through a junk yard.

Appliances: The 1950s retro look has been enhanced with up-to-the-minute appliances. Gleaming chrome and stainless steel make ideal partners for the metal units.

Windows: The gathered curtains and pelmets in floral-print fabric add a touch of old-fashioned romance to offset the hard metallics and bold flooring. They also add definition to the windows by framing them with color.

The look: Hot pink and vibrant geometric stripes bring a hint of lively psychedelic kitsch to a contemporary kitchen. All the color power comes from the walls, with white units and gleaming steel appliances offering a clean contrast.

Color: If you want a warm and stimulating kitchen, think pink. A hot shade like this will create an all-round glow. For a dramatically modern look, balance it with dazzling white units, then calm things down a little with neutral-colored flooring. The attention-grabbing stripes form a focal point in this room, adding a wacky dimension to the look with their bold pattern and mix of contrasting colors.

Striped cabinets: The painted stripes highlight the large MDF structure that incorporates the wall cabinets and surrounds the small window. Built from counter to ceiling, it provides cleverly disguised storage space, turns an insignificant window into a naturally lit display area and creates a striking feature for the room.

Units: The white, flat-fronted units with curvy chrome handles have clean, contemporary appeal. The work surface is made up of white mini mosaic tiles, dotted randomly with colored ones in pink, orange and silver. It curves out on either side to add flowing modern shape to the classic U-style layout.

Appliances: Colored fridges are popular, but if you plan to invest in a large, expensive model it may be wiser to avoid matching it exactly to a very distinctive color scheme. Stainless steel is more stylish than white, has sleek modern appeal and will team with any color if you redecorate. This fridge matches the steel oven, vent and splashback.

KITCHEN TIP
If you are painting designs such as stripes that require small amounts of several different paint shades, save money by using test pots of emulsion rather than larger cans

The look: Gentle retro shades of blue and green endow this kitchen with a laid-back mood, which is enhanced by its easy access to the garden and the natural appeal of its stripped floorboards.

Color: Pale, smoky blues and mint green form a harmonious combination. The walls are painted in a soothing shade of blue-grey, similar to that on the units, while the light green on the skirtings and door frames tones with the colored fridge. The window blind injects a sharper, citrus accent which is echoed by the splashback tiles. Natural tones and textures, in the wooden floorboards, basket of logs and terracotta pots, keep the look relaxed.

Units: The units have been revamped with a few coats of paint, the cheapest way of giving an existing kitchen a fresh new look. Details count, so don't forget to update the handles too – shiny chrome goes well with cool blue.

Floor: Stripped floorboards have a beautifully natural look and are also easy to clean, a practical choice for any room. If you have boards in good condition, all you need to do is strip and varnish them. Tackle this yourself by renting sanding machines from rental shops, who will explain how to use them. Seal the sanded floor by applying two coats of acrylic varnish.

Doors: Part of the end wall was knocked out in order to install a pair of glazed doors. As well as making the garden feel like part of the house, they allow far more light into the kitchen. A simple roller blind provides shade when necessary.

The look: An authentic 1950s look brings character to this spacious kitchen, which uses original metal units, Formica counters and retro-style cookware to recreate the style down to the last detail. Typical 1950s colors – zingy pistachio green and bright berry red – create a high-impact scheme.

Color: A large room can take strong colors, vibrant contrasts and bold patterns, and this kitchen has all three. Radiant red countertops provide a sizzling contrast with the sharp pistachio green that covers both the walls and units. Red also contrasts with freshening white, in lively checkerboard flooring that adds pattern and pace to the scheme. Sleek chrome and steel surfaces smarten the look with their reflective sheen.

Units: The 1950s metal kitchen units were rescued from a junk yard. After cleaning, the door fronts were painted using a process called powder coating, which dries to an ultra-smooth finish. The handles are painted red to match the counters, which have smoothly curved corners that echo the shape of the unit drawers. The countertops are made from that 1950s essential, Formica, which continues up onto the walls to form a small splashback.

Oven: This is a kitchen designed for serious food preparation, with a large, professional range oven. The stainless steel finish of the stove and curved extractor matches the drawer fronts.

Floor: Linoleum tiles are easy to lay, no trouble to clean, and allow you to combine two colors in this way to create a zappy checkerboard effect. It may overpower in a small room but is a cheerful way of enlivening a large floor area.

The look: A room that gets all-day sun is a perfect candidate for strong color, and apple green makes the most of the bright atmosphere. It gives this room a retro twist, which is reinforced by open shelving and 1950s accessories.

Color: Teamed with plenty of clean white, apple green creates a thoroughly refreshing environment. The sharpness of the wall color is softened by checkerboard floor tiles in gentler shades of green and off-white, and by accents of blue in countertops and accessories.

Furniture: The existing unit doors didn't suit the new look so the carcasses have been fitted with plainer ones. Painted white, these are topped with a durable pale blue Formica work surface. A round table fits more easily than a square one into the limited space beside the window. Shape adds style, and the table and chairs offset the straight lines of the units with flowing curves.

Shelving: A shelf unit sitting on the counter provides easily accessible storage, and adds visual interest to the expanse of plain wall. More shelves slot into alcoves beside this wall – to give them a chunkier look, they are edged with 6cm-wide MDF strips. All the shelving is painted white, to match the units.

Accessories: Brightly colored china and cookware complement the 1950s flavor. Other accessories have more obvious retro connections: the old-fashioned radio and coffee pots and the enamel advertising signs on the shelves and fridge epitomize the look.

KITCHEN TIP
A kitchen table can dominate a room, so choose one that leaves enough space to walk around. If your room is small, make sure chairs can fit neatly underneath the table when not in use

The look: Freestanding furniture painted in a selection of different colors gives this large kitchen an elegant semi-fitted look. The wide range cooker, traditional wooden plate rack and flagstone flooring add to its classic country-house style.

Color: In a large kitchen with lots of units, painting them in different colors helps to break the monotony, creating an individual look. This room's units contribute blocks of yellow ochre, duck-egg blue and aubergine which, together with the cream oven, make a colorful but sophisticated mix. The walls have been painted in a shade of yellow that is warm and welcoming but not so strong that it overpowers the other colors in the room. The brightly colored tiles above the range add pattern to an otherwise plain scheme.

Units: The handmade painted units are inspired by period styles and sold as freestanding individual pieces available in a range of colors and finishes. The distressed effect not only adds character but is also user-friendly – especially if you have young children –as it disguises any knocks and scratches. If there's enough space for it, a central island unit provides valuable extra work area and storage as well as creating a focal point for the room.

Countertops: Reinforcing the separate identity of each block of units, the work surfaces show an imaginative use of different natural materials: hard-wearing teak around the sink, warm-toned maple for the central island and dense slate on either side of the range.

Floor: The stone floor tiles have a mellow, aged appearance that complements the distressed finish of the units. Their impermeable surface makes them a practical choice for a family kitchen.

KITCHEN TIP
To distress wooden furniture, first paint it a light color. When dry, rub a candle on areas where natural wear might occur, such as panel edges. Paint with a deeper color. When dry, rub the waxed areas with steel wool to expose patches of base coat

The look: Unfinished brick-work around the stove, wooden storage racks and leafy plants give this kitchen an inviting country farmhouse feel, while the flamboyant Mediterranean colors pack punch into the look.

Color: Ultramarine blue and brilliant yellow form a stunning contrast that creates a vibrant, energetic atmosphere. For maximum impact, the two shades are equally balanced, with yellow paint on the walls and blue on the units. The glowing warmth of the yellow is matched by the earthy pinks and browns of the brickwork and wooden furniture.

Units: The blue finish on the units is the result of a paint job. The pine underneath was prepared for painting with a coat of multi-surface primer. Some wooden units can simply be sanded down to provide a key for the paint, but if they have a waxed or varnished finish, you will either need to remove this first or cover it with a suitable primer so that the top coat can adhere.

Wall racks: Carefully contrived clutter gives a country-style room a homey feel, so use open racks to keep some storage on show. Plate racks stacked with china, wine racks full of bottles and pans hanging from hooks all help to create the farmhouse effect.

Windows: For a totally rustic look, leave wooden window frames in their natural, unpainted state. These windows are dressed with Roman blinds featuring a pretty design of potted flowers, a neat reflection of the real plants displayed in front of them.

KITCHEN TIP
Many house plants thrive in the steamy and humid atmosphere of a kitchen, so use their lush foliage to enhance a country scheme or liven up a windowsill

bread
eggs
milk

The look: A modern kitchen with traditional touches sits comfortably in a Victorian house. The pale coloring looks fresh and contemporary, while an old pine dresser and wooden accessories sum up the casual, country atmosphere.

Color: The all-cream scheme gives the long kitchen a bright, airy feel, with the units, walls and flooring all in matching shades. Granite-effect counters add a welcome touch of deeper color, while the rich wood tones of the door and dresser are highlighted by contrast with the light backdrop.

Furniture: The simple detailing of the Shaker-style cupboards is in harmony with the age of the house, and a pale cream like this would typically have been used to lighten Victorian basement kitchens. A long run of units on either side of the room provides plenty of storage, and mixing plain, panelled, V-grooved and glass doors avoids a uniform look. Space has been left at one end for the old dresser, its wooden handles tying in with the knobs on the units.

Door: Although they are often overlooked, doors can do much to enhance the style of a room scheme if carefully chosen. This beautiful panelled model, found in an architectural junk yard, has been fitted with etched glass to allow light to filter through into the hallway beyond.

Floor: The original Victorian floorboards have been sanded, then given a New England-style finish with off-white paint. Varnish protects the paintwork, while natural matting punctuates the cool expanse with rustic color and texture.

The look: A mix of country and city styles, this kitchen teams traditional greens, wooden units and a big butler-style sink with up-to-the-minute ceiling spotlights and touches of chrome.

Color: As the color of nature, green is ideal for a country-style kitchen. Light shades, such as the soft apple used for the units, create an atmosphere that's both relaxing and refreshing, while darker olive tones, as on the stable-style door, have a reassuringly traditional feel. Yellow walls add warmth while keeping the overall look bright – two sandy shades have been applied as a colorwash to give the look of old plaster.

Units: The room's rural character derives from the tongue-and-groove panelled effect of the wooden units and the natural tone and texture of the iroko hardwood

countertops. A plate rack in matching wood allows for open storage and display – another hallmark feature of a country-style kitchen. Chrome knobs and handles give the overall look a modern edge. They are echoed by accessories and by the contemporary metal stool that allows the foreground unit to be used as a breakfast bar.

Oven vent: The wide range-style stove sits beneath an overmantel-cum-oven vent with curved, classic-style supports. This has been specially made from plywood and finished with a paint effect that makes it look like granite.

Sink: The porcelain sink not only suits the style of the room but is also wide enough to take the largest casserole dishes, an important consideration if you do a lot of cooking.

The look: Sun-baked shades of yellow and terracotta bring glowing Mediterranean color to this small kitchen, teaming up with birch units for a look that's light but warm.

Color: Yellow blends harmoniously with wood grain to create a warm, welcoming atmosphere. If you want to keep the look light and contemporary, choose blond wood units and a bright shade of yellow. Wall tiles in earthy tones of terracotta and sand give the scheme an exotic, sun-baked feel. These rich colors are repeated in the tableware and the small checks of the Roman blind.

Units: Ideal for an unfussy, contemporary look, the units are plain in style, with flat drawer fronts and simple Shaker-style panelling on the cupboards. Their quirky hammered-metal knobs also look stylishly modern. The birch units are topped with work surfaces made from

beech, an equally pale wood, and complemented by wooden dining furniture. The table is an antique store buy which required a lot of elbow grease to restore it to its former glory. The top was given a good sanding and rubbed down with fine steel wool, then treated with color-enhancing wax.

Splashback: The wall tiles, laid in a checkerboard pattern, have a weathered appearance which enhances the earthy nature of their colors. Pencil tiles add a defining line between the splashback and yellow walls. Using larger tiles can increase the impression of space in a small room.

Accessories: Tableware, mats and napkins reflect the color theme with shades of orange and yellow. Other accessories add natural texture and color, such as the basket, terracotta trough and cooking ingredients visible through clear glass jars.

The look: With a selection of old wooden furniture, plus floor tiles in a rich tone of terracotta, this kitchen-dinette is full of rustic warmth. The painted units and walls ensure that it's also wide awake with brilliant color.

Color: Yellow is a wonderful color for a dining area as it promotes sociability, and a stimulating shade is just the thing to cheer up a sluggish family first thing in the morning! The glazed floor tiles reflect its glow, their deep terracotta tones mingling with the yellow to radiate warmth throughout the room. Units painted in a vivid grass green provide a sharp contrast, while curtains in a colorful country check pull together the green and yellow, teaming it with accents of red.

Units: The wooden units have been built to fit around the butler's sink, then painted. Modern metal handles, although at odds with the room's country character, suit their simple styling. The cherrywood countertop reflects the rich colors of the floor tiles and older woods.

Wooden furniture: The tables and chairs all come from antique shops and auctions, and their mixture of styles enhances the room's informal feel. Units are fitted along one wall only, allowing freestanding pieces to contribute character.

Floor: As well as having a beautiful shine, glazed ceramic tiles are completely resistant to staining and need only regular washing to remain in tiptop condition. However, they are also cold underfoot and show no mercy to dropped dishes.

The look: An all-cream backdrop combats the potentially gloomy effect of this room's low ceiling and dark beams to ensure a light, contemporary environment. A more creative use of color makes a focal point of the dining furniture.

Color: If you want to make a small or dingy room seem as bright and spacious as possible, use a pale neutral to cover the walls and larger furnishings. In a kitchen, this means choosing light-colored units and wall tiles to match. Cream is a softer choice than brilliant white, and easier to live with when used in large doses. By using it to guarantee a light look, you can then liven things up with small amounts of brighter color. In this room the curtains and dining furniture offer the chance for color fun, while terracotta-toned floor tiles and wooden countertops add a touch of natural warmth.

Units: To keep the background streamlined, the units have a plain, modern design with Shaker-style panelling, and the oven vent is incorporated into the wall-cupboard structure. Simple door and drawer knobs match the blond wood of the counters.

Dining furniture: As a lighthearted design statement, the individual chairs of the dining set have been painted in different colors. This also introduces a lively mix of hues to brighten up the cream scheme. The fresh contemporary shades of orange, yellow, lilac and blue are picked out from the squared design on the tabletop.

Window: A further splash of color is provided by the pretty turquoise curtain, consisting of a simple tab-top panel that is sheer enough to let plenty of natural light filter through its fabric.

The look: A bold contrast between rich terracotta and cool cream gives this kitchen as smart a look as the dining room it leads into. Shaker-style units, wooden worktops and a butler's sink set the tone for country-house style.

Color: A deep shade of terracotta is a brave choice for both the walls and flooring, but the room is large and bright enough to benefit from this strong, dark color. The cream units and splashback tiles freshen the overall effect. The warm, natural feel created by the terracotta is enhanced by the bright wood tones of the butcher's block and counters.

Dining area: In an open-plan room, using different decor in each area helps to give them separate identities. The walls of the dining space are panelled with oak-veneered MDF, which is sealed with Danish oil and acrylic varnish. The floor area beneath the table and chairs is covered with a sisal mat.

Units: The units have been created using cheap off-the-rack carcasses and custom-made MDF doors, painted in cream. The base units have unfussy Shaker-style panelling, while chicken wire adds a country touch to the open-fronted wall units. The counter is made from solid oak. A mobile butcher's block makes use of the large central floor area to provide additional storage space as well as an extra work surface.

Floor: Vinyl floor tiles are hard-wearing and easy to clean. If you like the natural look of stone or ceramic tiling but want something that's more practical and comfortable underfoot, vinyl lookalikes could be the answer. This flooring is designed to imitate quarry tiles.

The look: Spanish wall tiles and sea-fresh shades of blue and green combine with rustic open brickwork and natural wood to create a country look with a Mediterranean flavor.

Color: Although blue is a cool colour, some of its brighter mid-tone shades are perfect for creating a heartwarming, summery feel. Sky shades and clear aquas give a refreshing lift to the natural tones and textures of materials such as wood and brick. White brightens the look further, its clean contrast with the blues and greens of the walls and counter tiles bringing to mind the brilliance of white-walled Greek villages. The Spanish wall tiles are an authentic Mediterranean touch, and their navy borders add definition to the splashback.

Sink: The butler's sink, traditional feature of a country kitchen, sits within a specially built brick surround fitted with a wooden door at the front to allow access for plumbing

purposes. Open brickwork will give a particularly rustic look to any room.

Countertops: Covering counters with ceramic tiles allows you to create decorative and colorful effects. In this room mottled blues and greens have been arranged in a checkerboard pattern and are surrounded by a wooden trim. Although the grout may be hard to keep clean, tiled counters are heat and water-resistant – look for tiles with a glaze that won't discolor. Rather than forming part of a fitted design, this surface stands alone, providing ample work area while allowing freestanding furniture and appliances to slide underneath.

Accessories: Blue and green tableware introduces more Mediterranean colors, while simple wooden accessories enhance the room's rustic character. Chrome offsets the natural look with a contemporary glimmer.

KITCHEN TIP
Butler's sinks can be bought new, but try junk yards for well-priced original designs. Look in your phone book or on the Internet for junk yards in your area

The look: Rustic charm gets the designer treatment in a dramatic scheme dominated by wood, stone and metal. Unique furniture fashioned from chunky wood sits against a backdrop of exposed stone walls, while stainless steel appliances and cookware add a high-tech glint.

Color: Most of the room's color comes from natural materials. The unfinished grey stone of the far wall creates a cave-like atmosphere, which is warmed by the richer browns of the wooden furniture, beams and flooring. Texture is as important as color in creating the rustic feel, with rough stone, polished wood grain and smooth metal forming a fascinating mix of surfaces. The side walls are painted in green which, with its natural associations, is a good choice to complement this decor.

Furniture: Wooden countertops that look as if they have been hewn straight from the trunk run around the walls of the kitchen. Unit doors in similar wood provide covered storage around the stove, but most of the area underneath is left open to enhance the informal character of the look. The cherrywood table with wrought-iron legs makes an arresting centerpiece, although a selection of mismatched wooden chairs strikes a more casual note.

Splashback: A band of tiles creates a narrow splashback. Their mosaic-style animal designs suit the natural theme of the room and echo its neutral tones.

Pot rack: The glimmer of metal pans and appliances provides a sleek contrast for the wood and stone. In an original take on the traditional country-style pot rack, a metal holder with contemporary curves gives pans a chance to shine.

The look: Give country style an up-to-date edge by teaming natural wood and wicker with light colors. This room's dark timber beams dictate a rustic flavor for its furnishings, but cream units and yellow walls ensure that the atmosphere remains bright and airy.

Color: Cream is a versatile neutral that ranges in character from richly classic to coolly contemporary. When used on wooden units it gives a modern-country feel, soft enough to complement the glowing tones of the mellow wooden counters, yet pale enough to keep the whole room feeling light and spacious. The yellow colorwash on the walls heightens this brightening effect, joining the brilliant blues of the splashback tiles to add a dash of Mediterranean color.

Units: The simple design of the base units suits the contemporary freshness of the room. Glass-fronted wall cupboards give a lighter look than solid doors and allow you to show off attractive glassware or china. The oven, range and island work surface are designed to be within easy reach of each other. Pine stools pull up to the island for casual meals, while wicker baskets slide into the modular shelf spaces beneath to provide country-style storage. Beech work surfaces add warm, natural color to the scheme.

Splashback: The colorful Spanish-style tiles that cover the splashback include about six different shades of blue, yellow and cream. If you want to attempt a random arrangement of several colors, it's a good idea to draw a plan on paper before you start, showing which tiles should go where in order to achieve a good mix.

The look: There's never a dull day in this kitchen, where yellow blends with mellow wood to create a scheme bursting with warmth and energy. An abundance of natural color and texture creates an atmosphere of cosy rural charm.

Color: Warm colors, whether in paint shades or wood tones, can't fail to create a welcoming environment, and can work wonders in a chilly, north-facing room. However, they should be used with caution in a tiny kitchen as they could make it seem smaller. This room is dominated by the deep orange tones of the wooden furniture and flooring. The equally strong shade of yellow matches its intensity to raise the temperature still further, while bringing out the glowing tones of the grain.

Units: If you love the beauty and warmth of wood grain, oak is a classic choice for a kitchen.

With unfussy panelling and simple white knobs, these solid-framed units would be plain enough to suit a more contemporary setting, but they also look perfectly at home alongside the old wooden dresser.

Dresser: As well as adding country character, a traditional dresser is an extremely useful piece of furniture, providing floor-to-ceiling storage, plus work surface and display areas. Hooks inserted in the front edge of one shelf show off a collection of decorative jugs.

Window: While perking up the scheme with a band of pattern, the yellow checks of the Roman blind tone closely with the walls for a totally coordinated look. The terracotta pots lining the sill add to the earthy colors and rustic atmosphere of the room.

KITCHEN TIP
Wood color changes over time, and some grains darken quicker than others. Remember to check with your kitchen supplier how the appearance of wooden units may be affected

The look: A roomful of pine cupboards oozes rustic charm, but can seem dated and unimaginative. Transforming them with colored paint gives a fashionable look without the need for refitting, and dark green retains their country character while lending it a more formal edge.

Color: Teaming comfortably with wood tones, the somber green gives this room a cosy, traditional feel. Yellow walls brighten the look, but choosing a mellow shade keeps the mood relaxed. Country checks make an appearance in the seat cushions and the pelmet above the window, jazzing up the scheme a little with accents of red and orange.

Furniture: The pine units have been painted with an oil-based eggshell. Although natural pine might seem overwhelming when used for built-in cabinets, it will always find a place in a country-style scheme; the sturdy table and bench provide a warm, homey focus for casual meals, homework or any number of other family activities. The garden-style bench emphasizes the rural feel of the room, and gets a comfort boost from seat and throw cushions.

Window: Leaving the wide window without blinds or curtains shows off the elegant wooden frames, lets in the maximum amount of daylight and makes the most of the garden view. The narrow pelmet of checked fabric is enough to give the window a dressed look, adding a decorative band of color and pattern without obscuring the panes.

Floor: Laminate beech-effect flooring gives the appearance of wood at a fraction of the price. It is actually made from printed paper glued onto timber and sealed with a resin finish. Laminate flooring is stain- and heat-resistant and is easy to keep clean.

The look: Converting a Victorian dining room into a kitchen can mean fitting units into awkward spaces, but the advantage here is the large windows, which flood the room with light and offer a broad view of the garden while doing the washing-up.

Color: The original brick fireplace sets the tone for a traditional look, which the muted colors help to reinforce. A buttery yellow reflects the abundant natural daylight and offsets the dark brickwork. Cool eau de nil has been used to pick out the window frames and picture rail as well as paint the units, thereby coordinating the room's fittings with its furniture. The dark metal of the unit handles and the steely tones of the stove echo the slate-grey countertops.

Units: As windows extend along most of one wall, leaving little space for cupboards, a long central island has been built to house most of the units, and even the sink. Narrow wall and base cupboards are squeezed into the alcove beside the chimney breast, while the range cooker occupies the space left by the fireplace.

The units are made up of cheap carcasses fitted with custom-made Shaker-style door fronts, which can be supplied ready to paint.

Countertops: The counters are also homemade. Cut from MDF, they have been painted black, then finished with a mixture of varnish and graphite powder to create a slate effect.

Accessories: To complete the traditional country look, old-fashioned accessories can often be found at markets and antiques fairs. The enamelled tin bread box and patterned china butter dish, for example, were picked up quite cheaply.

The look: Brimming with color and character, this kitchen is as much of a showcase for quirky treasures as it is a place for preparing food. Open storage units and highly decorative wall tiles create an individual look.

Color: Blocks of soft color work well together. The warm pink walls and toning floor tiles make the overall atmosphere cosy and inviting, and the dark woods of the units and shelves create a more traditional feel. Lighter contrasts come from the cream Aga and pale green retro-style fridge, while the sharper greens and jazzy patterns of the splashback tiles give the room a Mexican flavor. The bowls and other ornaments displayed on the shelves add further bright color as well as a rich variety of patterns.

Furniture: If you don't like the uniform appearance of built-in units, go for a more casual look with open-fronted storage.

Shelves beneath the counter accommodate pots and pans, and country-style wicker baskets can be added to help you store smaller items in an orderly fashion. For individual style, consider using furniture that might look more at home in a living room or bedroom, such as the small wall cabinet in the corner of this kitchen, which is used to store frequently used ingredients.

Accessories: The colorful collection of bowls, books, ornaments and glassware makes this kitchen feel like an Aladdin's cave, an impression enhanced by the magical twinkle of the lights strung along the top of the window frames. The treasures are displayed on open shelves that run the entire length of the walls, even covering the small windows.

KITCHEN TIP
Range cookers now come in a number of different colors, and slimline models are also available. These share the traditional looks and specialist cooking functions of original designs while fitting into smaller kitchens

The look: A combination of retro style and modern-country cool brings character to this kitchen-dinette. The large room provides space for individual touches such as the collection of colorful pottery and the 1950s American jukebox that sits beside the Aga.

Color: With soft cream on the walls and Edwardian-style green on the units, the scheme has a traditional air, and the natural wood of the long table and chairs adds to its country-house feel. The cream and green contrast is highlighted by the Mexican wall tiles, where the two shades combine in a lively checkerboard pattern. The cream walls make a plain foil for the bright pottery, which adds accents of orange, blue and yellow.

Units: This previously all-white kitchen needed color to warm it up, so the existing units have been revamped with green paint and fitted with old-fashioned metal handles. The white counters have been replaced with dark wood for a more relaxed look.

Splashback: An element of pattern adds pace and interest, especially in a large room, and tiles in a checkerboard design are an easy way of introducing it. The coordinating tiles with leaf motifs, fitted in the alcove above the Aga, break up the geometric effect.

Accessories: Curvy chrome accessories evoke 1950s style. Chrome lamps hang low over the table, while shiny small appliances grace the worktop. Open shelves display more colorful accessories: Clarice Cliff and Susie Cooper china, plus bright mugs and glass jars of cooking ingredients.

The look: Salsa into the kitchen for a little fiesta. Take your decor down Mexico way with hot pinks and guacamole green, metal surfaces and rustic terracotta flooring. Then have fun stacking brightly painted shelves with kitsch accessories and colorful retro memorabilia.

Color: Bold clashing colors such as pink and green are a key ingredient of this look, so use them liberally on walls, shelving and accessories. For true Mexican style, add a geometric decoration along the shelf edges. However, don't overdo the sizzling style; it's a look you may tire of, so choose more versatile colors for units and countertops. Cupboards painted in pale blue and worktops in a darker shade add to the multicolored effect while providing a cool balance for the hot brights.

Metallics: Punched or recycled tin is a feature of Mexican art, so use it on anything from doors to picture frames. For a more modern interpretation, capture the spirit of the look with smooth metal surfaces. Here a gleaming stainless steel fridge and oven are joined by a metal chair. The splashback tiles are decorated with metallic spray paint.

Floor: Terracotta floor tiles acknowledge the rustic side of Mexican style, although these are sealed and polished to give them a sheen almost as bright as the metal surfaces.

Accessories: Small appliances and tableware in zingy colors are widely available, and we've all got pieces of brightly painted pottery tucked away. To make the look even more convincing, search out Mexican-style pictures, frames and ornaments. Striped fabrics in many colors recall ponchos – use them to make tea towels and napkins.

The look: Funky lozenge shapes and a blend of subtle retro colors spring from looks dating back half a century to create a 1950s-inspired kitchen with fresh modern appeal.

Color: Steering clear of the zingy brights often associated with 1950s style, this room uses softer shades from the retro palette to create a more calming environment. Baby blue walls, lavender units and taupe flooring make a harmonious mix which boasts plenty of color but no disturbing contrasts.

Furniture: The units have been decorated using melamine primer followed by satin-finish lavender paint. The table is a 1950s original, found in a antique shop, but has been promoted to family size with a larger MDF top fitted over the existing one and painted to match the units. The chairs, also antique store buys, have been updated with taupe paint and linen seat covers. Adding exciting texture to the room, the rugged cushion covers are made from bath mats dyed baby blue.

Wall shelf: The display shelf reinforces the 1950s theme with its evocative lozenge shape and, as the only wall unit, makes an eye-catching feature. Painted to match the chairs and floor, it is made from 2in-thick MDF and flexible plywood, which can be bent into curves.

Floor: Think twice before ripping up tatty linoleum – if it's worn but not torn you can paint over it. You need a floor paint formulated for use on vinyl, available from DIY stores. This floor has been given three coats of taupe paint, which is topped with a dark blue lozenge pattern that echoes the shape of the wall shelf.

The look: This kitchen has the look of an expensive handmade design, but is actually made up of end-of-range units bought from three different stores. A clever makeover with cream paint has turned them into a matching set, creating a charming country-style kitchen for a period house.

Color: The plain cream scheme is designed to complement the rustic wooden ceiling beams, an original feature of the room. Rich cream has traditional appeal, and provides a clean but gentle foil for the beauty of natural wood. The chunky wooden countertops echo the honeyed tones of the beams.

Units: Units from discontinued lines can often be picked up at bargain prices. These were discovered as display models in three different stores; although the design is the same, each store's batch had a different paint finish. In order to have enough units to fill their kitchen, the owners bought the lot and stripped them back to the bare wood. Having fitted the units, they then primed, undercoated and applied cream satin-finish paint to give them a seamless look. White ceramic knobs add the finishing touch.

Splashback: To continue the painted-wood look throughout the kitchen, the splashback is covered with country-style tongue-and-groove panels, painted to match the units.

Plate rack: There weren't quite enough units to cover the wall above the sink, so a plate rack has been made to fill the gap. Painted to blend in with the units, it adds to the room's traditional character.

The look: A low-budget makeover gives a stark white kitchen a cosier atmosphere. Bright red paint brings a glow to the walls, cork tiles add natural warmth at floor level and strips of brown vinyl provide a color cure for the clinical-looking units.

Color: Cool colors recede, making a room feel airier, but warm hues such as red and orange will appear to advance towards you, creating a more intimate atmosphere. That's why they are ideal for warming up a kitchen full of white units and wall tiles, where the freshness of the white balances the strong red, preventing it from seeming overpowering. Cork floor tiles and wooden countertops add further warm color while softening the strong contrast between the red and white, their natural tones giving the room a more relaxed feel.

Units: To stop the white units

from looking too stark against the red walls, a strip of self-adhesive vinyl has been stuck across each door. The wood-grain effect matches the natural texture of the counter and table, while its darker brown provides a stronger balance for the bold lipstick red.

Storage racks: If you're short on storage but can't afford extra units, look for cheap freestanding racks that can accommodate surplus crockery or foodstuffs. The white plastic corner unit fits neatly in place at the end of the run of units. Wall racks are also useful for hanging utensils.

Window: If red walls make your room feel smaller and darker, a white Venetian blind might provide a solution. It lets natural light flow between its slats, and in this room matches the units.

KITCHEN TIP
Give a white fridge or washing machine a colorful makeover by covering it with shapes cut from sticky-backed plastic. You can also buy spray paints designed for decorating appliances

The look: If a kitchen is visible from the living and dining areas, you can either make a feature of it with color or keep the decor understated so that it fades into the background. This one goes for the latter option, with plain white units and tiles that blend with the walls of the main room.

Color: Although white rules, it is punctuated by strong accent colors that add impact to the overall look. The strip of orange wall above the units is enough to make the room feel bright and cheerful rather than boring. The black countertops tone with the grey metallics of the bin and stainless steel accessories to give a smart, sophisticated feel.

Units: With flat doors as plain as they come, these units score high for contemporary simplicity. Long metal handles enhance their sleek looks. Choosing a white oven to match the units gives the kitchen a thoroughly uniform, streamlined appearance.

Lighting: Good lighting is essential in a kitchen, especially one without windows. A track system attached to the ceiling can support a number of lights that provide more efficient and focused illumination than a single pendant lamp. These three adjustable spotlights can be directed onto different parts of the work surface to light up even the darkest corners.

Accessories: The accessories fit the color theme, with pans and bowls in black and white, plus an orange kettle that echoes the wall color. Checked tea towels introduce bold pattern to sharpen up the plain scheme. Stainless steel appliances add to the slick, modern feel of the room, and even the galvanized bin has utility chic.

KITCHEN TIP
Lighting should never be an afterthought, particularly in a kitchen, so plan your lighting at the same time as your layout. Also, remember to consider whether you need extra outlets for appliances

The look: With dried chillies hanging from the shelves, an Indian wallhanging in the dining area and a mixture of zingy colors, this kitchen has a vibrant, ethnic air.

Color: Lush green makes a bold color statement on the units. The walls are white, to avoid overwhelming the space with color, but painting a few splash-back tiles dark blue adds a second bold shade to offset the sizzling green. The mosaic tiles and tableware add accents of lime, red and blue to brighten the effect further.

Furniture: Traditional wooden units get an instant update with a coat of boldly colored paint. These panelled doors and drawers are also fitted with new cup handles. The beech countertop and wooden furniture evoke a rustic feel that works well with the ethnic accessories. A decorative shelf unit, used as a spice rack, adds an individual touch above the sink area, while a chunky wooden table and mismatched chairs help to set the scene for casual dining.

Sink: The humble sink isn't often a focal point, but covering the surround with inexpensive mosaic tiles has turned this one into an eye-catching feature. A handful of bright tiles creates a lively effect when interspersed with fresh white ones.

Splashback: The blue tiles are decorated with spray paint so as not to show any brushstrokes. Mask off the surrounding tiles well and brush on tile primer. When dry, apply the spray paint in light coats so that it doesn't run.

The look: This might look like a designer kitchen but the units are 1930s antique store finds, cleverly updated to suit this cool, modern environment. Economizing on cupboards left cash free to splash out on a specially made stainless steel extractor, which entices the eye up beyond the rafters to form an impressive focal point for this massive room.

Color: Cream-painted floorboards and walls maximize the illusion of space, and reflective steel and glass surfaces bounce light around, making the room feel even more airy. The aquamarine units add contemporary color, while the brighter blues of the rug and chair covers mark out the dining area.

Units: The units are made from 1930s-style cupboards, revamped with colored paint. A plinth at the bottom adjusts their heights to give an even work surface, and they are linked, visually and structurally, by pilasters made from stair spindles sawn in half. An island unit provides a convenient surface for the range. Like the extractor, the counters are made from brushed stainless steel, and their shiny surface is echoed by the metal handles of the units.

Dining furniture: The unusual dining table is another home-made creation. The legs are made from turned wood decorated with silver gilding, which gives them a Michelin-Man-goes-space-age look. The wicker chairs add a natural touch among the kitchen's cool colors and metal fittings.

Window: The large windows are dressed with Venetian blinds, which provide an effective form of light control as the slats are fully adjustable. When horizontal, they let in the maximum amount of natural light to keep the room bright and airy.

KITCHEN TIP
Brushed stainless steel is a more practical choice for countertops and splashbacks than the smooth, shinier variety as its texture helps to conceal scratches

The look: Bright blues chase the cobwebs from an outdated kitchen to create a refreshing contemporary look. Only the mosaic-tiled countertop and unit handles are new – the rest of the old kitchen remains, hidden beneath some nifty paintwork.

Color: Cool and uplifting, aqua blue is perfect for an upbeat modern scheme. Used on both the walls and units, with white splashback tiles to provide a fresh contrast, it brightens up the entire room. The mosaic tiles on the counter add a slightly Mediterranean feel. Their tiny squares introduce pattern interest as well as a medley of harmonizing colors to offset the plain blocks of blue and white.

Units: With fresh aqua paint bringing them right up to date, the panelled wooden units have lost their heavy, traditional look. Their old, outdated handles are also gone, replaced with sleek brushed-metal designs.

Countertop: The countertop's mosaic tiles are laid on top of its original grey Formica. Mosaics are not as fiddly to apply as you might think; craft stores sell sheets of tiles attached to backing paper, to save gluing them in place one by one. However, bear in mind that the thin tiles are more decorative than durable when used on a counter – for example, they might not stand up to the impact inflicted by heavy pots and pans.

Splashback: White tile paint, applied over a suitable primer, has been used to freshen up the splashback. A few of the tiles have also been decorated with a diamond design, created by masking off the shape and then painting it with the same colors used on the walls and units. This helps to pull the color scheme together.

KITCHEN TIP
Whatever material you choose for counters, always prepare food on cutting boards rather than directly on top of the counter. As well as being more hygienic, this protects the surface from scratches and stains

The look: A new kitchen is no more costly than some MDF and a can of paint. Instead of replacing your units, fit DIY doors for a brand-new look, and save a little money for stylish fittings, appliances and accessories.

Color: A combination of soft blue, white and dark brown is a modern classic, and makes a sophisticated-looking kitchen. The walls are painted in a slightly paler shade of blue than the units to create a soothing backdrop. The natural browns of the teak flooring and stained counter introduce a gentle farmhouse feel, enhanced by the country-style checks of the tablecloth. Accents of darker color, in the chairs and plum-colored tableware, add depth to the pale scheme.

Units: Flat MDF doors provide a blank canvas for whatever color you fancy – the choice is only as limited as the range of paint shades. Use your existing doors as a template to make new ones. Measure them, and ask a timber merchant or DIY store to cut 2cm MDF to size. Unscrew the old hinges (you should be able to re-use them) and use the doors as a pattern to help you mark hinge positions on the MDF. Designer-style fittings give a lift to basic doors – these long D-ring handles look stylishly modern.

Countertop: The wooden counter has been customized with a dark brown stain, then finished with a coat of matte varnish. A new sink and taps will update your kitchen – choose rounded designs for an easy-on-the-eye contemporary look.

Splashback: Sheets of laminated glass make a practical splashback that complements the delicate shades of blue. Fix the glass in place with mirror screws at each corner.

The look: Basic white units are the least expensive option from any supplier, but can be transformed with paint to give you your own unique look. Once you've got the framework of the kitchen looking good, you can introduce inexpensive fittings, flooring and work surfaces without compromising the room's style.

Color: Using a selection of different colors on unit doors and drawers creates an original look. Blue lends itself well to this idea as its shades mix particularly harmoniously – simply take a look at a strip of blue paint shades and pick out a handful of dark, light and mid tones. For slick contemporary style, team blues with silvery metals and fresh white countertops and appliances. The cork floor tiles add a touch of warmer color.

Units: The most affordable units are usually made from melamine, and in order to paint these you will need to begin with a melamine primer, to provide a key for the top coat. Apply two coats of primer, leaving each to dry for at least 16 hours. Then use good-quality gloss or eggshell paints in your chosen colors to give your units a total transformation.

Wall storage: Open storage cubes are cheaper and look more contemporary than wall cupboards. Stack them to make the best use of wall space, and use them to display your favorite items.

Splashback: A metal splashback has up-to-the-minute industrial style as well as reflective shine. Find a sheet metal company that will cut galvanized metal to your measurements – it will be cheaper than aluminium. Fix it securely to the wall with contact adhesive.

KITCHEN TIP
Cork is one of the best-value floorcoverings and is comfy in a room where you spend hours standing. Buy unfinished tiles and coat them with layers of cork tile sealant or hardwearing varnish. A matte finish gives a more modern effect

The look: Vivid blue forms a bold contrast with cream to bring striking color to this small kitchen. At the same time, using it to cover walls, tiles and units ensures a streamlined look.

Color: Giving your kitchen a complete paint job allows you to use the same shade on many different surfaces – tiles, units and walls. This gives a tiny kitchen a uniform feel and, if you choose a bright, bold color, can look dramatically modern. To avoid over-powering the room, include a block of lighter color: here the cream shelf unit balances the deep blue, and the tableware and ingredients within it add their own color accents, thereby softening the overall effect.

Units: In a small room, wall shelving gives a more airy, space-enhancing look than cupboards, and also keeps commonly used ingredients conveniently within reach for cooking rather than hidden away in deep cupboards. However, putting foodstuffs on display also demands orderly storage and frequent tidying to prevent shelves becoming a jumbled mess!

Tiles: Blue paint has transformed the wall and countertop tiles, which were once chilly white. Before painting tiles, apply a coat of multi-surface or tile primer, as ordinary paints will not adhere to the shiny surface. Follow this with a top coat of gloss, or use special tile paints.

Storage jars: Glass canisters not only make it easy to see at a glance what's where, but also allow ingredients such as rice and pasta to enliven a plain scheme with natural color and texture. Labels are a good idea, though – if only to distinguish sugar from salt!

The look: A few cosmetic improvements can lift a shabby kitchen out of the doldrums in a matter of days. A lick of color, some snappy steel panelling and a bit of neat tilework have turned this kitchen from grotty to great.

Color: The room's stainless steel oven, sink and toaster suggested a hi-tech look, so more steely surfaces have been introduced to boost the metallic effect. A pale watery blue keeps the look cool, but adds much-needed color to the room, freshening the effect created by the hard metals and stark white tiles.

Furniture: The units are painted with satinwood, in a shade that matches the emulsion used on the walls, and covered with panels of stainless steel. Ask a metal company to cut the steel to size, then fix it to the doors with strong adhesive. Prop up the bottom edge with panel pins to prevent it slipping while the glue dries. The dining table is also covered with sheet steel. Galvanized metal boxes add to the metallic elements in the room and smarten up the open-fronted unit by providing tidy storage for its contents.

Countertop: To bring color to the counter area, the tatty old countertop has been replaced with tiles in a pale aqua, which echoes the wall shade. A small work surface can be tiled quickly and easily, especially if you use fast-drying adhesive.

Splashback: The existing white tiles fit in well with the fresh new look, especially since their dirty grout has been retouched. This can be done in minutes using a grout pen, available from DIY stores.

The look: If you're revamping an existing kitchen, don't worry too much about following one particular style. Some of the most individual rooms are those that simply reflect the owner's personal tastes. This kitchen combines an adventurous use of color on the units with elaborately patterned wall tiles, and includes a mixture of old-fashioned and more modern accessories.

Color: Painting existing units gives you the chance to make a bold color statement, and using two contrasting shades can help to break up a run of cupboards, lending the overall look greater interest and impact. These cupboards, originally in shiny pine, are painted with vibrant hues which cheer up the room tremendously. While offsetting the darkening effect of the deep blue splashback, their bright shades of green and yellow also tone with the colors in the vegetable design of the patterned tiles, giving the scheme a unified look.

Units: If you want to paint varnished pine units, either sand them down very well to remove the varnish, or apply a multi-surface primer before painting. If you decide to go for a two-color effect on panelled units, use the lighter or brighter of the two shades to highlight the inner part of the panels. These units have golden cup handles and door knobs that echo the traditional feel of the pine counters and patterned tiles.

Accessories: Reflecting the contemporary versus classic feel of the decor, the accessories juxtapose old with new. Small appliances with zingy colors and modern curves share worktop space with an old-fashioned enamel bread box and china canisters.

The look: White tiles and units may seem bland but they'll go with any other color, and using a bold shade on the walls will give them an instant lift. Brilliant Mediterranean blue and brightly flowered curtains revitalize this tiny kitchen with a shot of color power.

Color: Why paint units or wall tiles when you can simply slap a bit of color on the walls? White fittings look clean and modern, and form a dazzling contrast with bright hues. As long as your wall area is not cluttered with cupboards, covering it with a vibrant shade will balance the white fittings, counteracting their clinical feel and working with them to give the room a fresh, feelgood atmosphere. Deep Mediterranean shades are particularly effective. This rich turquoise wall color is joined by the splashy pinks, greens and blues in the curtain print, and by bold yellow and orange accents in the plates mounted above the window.

Window: Although blinds are more practical near sinks as they trap less grime and roll up out of the way of splashes, curtains give a softer look. This gathered style with pleated pelmet frames the small window, turning it into a focal point. The print adds impact to the scheme by adding jazzy pattern and color, its big blooms suggesting a tropical feel.

Wall racks: Wall cupboards can make a small kitchen feel cramped, but racks and open units are a useful alternative. In a room with limited work surface, a wall-mounted spice holder keeps seasonings handy for cooking while leaving the tops clear. The corner unit has a more decorative, open look than a closed cupboard.

KITCHEN TIP
Kitchen window dressings will probably need washing more frequently than those elsewhere, so make sure blinds or curtains are easy to remove and replace

The look: Squeezed into a windowless corner of an open-plan room, this kitchen needed a colorful makeover, both to brighten it up and to improve the view from the living and dining areas.

Color: In a room with yellow walls the sun never stops shining, so it's an obvious choice to cheer up a dark space. Here it's teamed with mint and pistachio green, which give a fashionable 1950s retro feel. Accessories in yellow and silvery metallics keep the look smart and simple, while beechwood flooring adds a more natural touch.

Units: These units were originally white but looked too utilitarian for the multipurpose room. Color gives them a more dressy look; mint-green paint has transformed the doors and drawers, and long curved metal handles add a stylish finishing touch. New laminate countertops in pistachio green complete the color show. The white fridge-freezer is disguised by a wooden panel with cutout squares.

Splashback: Removing old wall tiles is a horrid job, and replacing them can be pricey, but that doesn't mean you have to live with them. Painting is an option, but even easier is covering them with another material. This splashback is covered with sheets of yellow laminate, glued onto the existing tiles.

Microwave: If you have a small household, a range and a microwave may meet all your cooking needs. In this kitchen, replacing the old oven with a microwave has created space underneath for a deep drawer, useful for storing pans. Building in a microwave beneath the countertop gives a streamlined look, but make sure you allow for ventilation.

The look: Wooden-spoon handles add a touch of humor to this country-style kitchen. Like the units, countertops and dining table, they are the result of a combination of creative thinking and clever DIY improvisation.

Color: Green gives a room a fresh outdoor look, and is used on these walls in its palest form to impart a country air while keeping the overall environment light and bright. The contrasting rich red has greater impact, drawing the eye directly to the units and outlining the traditional-style window. It tones with the terracotta floor tiles to give the room a warm, homely feel.

Units: The unit doors, fitted onto existing carcasses, are home-made from MDF and painted red. Their design, with a wide border panel and a diagonal strip across the center, is reminiscent of a stable door, enhancing the room's rustic flavor. Each wooden-spoon handle is fixed in place with two tiny pieces of dowel glued to the back. New countertops cut from timber have been treated with oil to seal and protect the wood.

Table: The dining table has been fitted with a new top, made to match the color scheme. Fashioned from scaffolding planks, it is painted in the same light green as the walls and fixed with screws to the old tabletop.

Door: In a traditionally styled kitchen, it can be difficult to make modern essentials such as fridges blend in. Here the fridge-freezer is hidden from view behind a floor-to-ceiling surround, made from plasterboard on a wooden frame and painted to blend in with the walls. A tall panelled door with old-fashioned hinges allows access.

The look: If you've inherited an uninspiring kitchen, the easiest way to perk it up is by painting the walls in a bold color. The neutral-toned units in this room suggested a natural look, with forest-green walls complemented by wooden furnishings and stone-effect flooring.

Color: Many people shy away from using strong shades, afraid that they'll look brash, but dark green adds color without drama. Restful and easy on the eye, it is often seen as traditional in character, but works just as well in a contemporary setting if freshened by plenty of white and lighter neutrals. In this room pale woods stand out against the dark walls while enhancing the natural quality of the green. Warmer tones come from the terracotta vase and countertop tiles, while the yellow walls of the hallway glimpsed through the open door add a brighter touch.

Countertops: Tiling the surfaces of both the existing units and the newly introduced wooden table has given the furniture a more coordinated look. The terracotta tiles add to the natural color in the room and provide a warming contrast beside the plain white splashback tiles.

Window: If you want a cheap window dressing with natural good looks, a pinoleum blind is the answer. Made up of narrow slats of wood, it allows sufficient light to filter through and keep the room bright.

Floor: Vinyl flooring is also reasonably priced, and many designs mimic natural wood or stone. This sheet flooring is made to look like stone tiles, and its neutral tones blend well with the color of the units.

The look: A large kitchen can handle strong color, and there's no more powerful combination than deep raspberry red and sharp yellow. Together they create a warm, stimulating atmosphere in this high-ceilinged Victorian room.

Color: Dramatic red dominates the room, used to cover both the walls and splashback tiles, while the yellow paintwork on the chair and units tones with the mellow wood of the dining table and bench. Black accents, in the skirting tiles and accessories, add a smart touch. The mottled grey and white squares of the vinyl floorcovering provide a softer neutral base for the room's vibrant colors, while jazzing up the large floor area with their checkerboard pattern.

Units: The wooden units have been painted in yellow, which forms a vivid contrast with the red walls. Using such a bright shade on a long run of base units might have seemed overpowering, but these cupboards are interspersed with white appliances which lend a fresher look to the overall scheme. Simple wooden knobs echo the pine table and bench.

Dining furniture: The chunky wooden table, with its unfinished wood grain and turned legs, brings a farmhouse feel to the kitchen, adding a relaxed, natural touch amid the striking colors. The wooden bench on the right also has rustic charm, but red cushions make for a comfier seating experience.

Accessories: Dotted around the walls, accessories help to break up the expanses of red. There's plenty of room for decorative items, like the large print and china fish, as well as more practical features such as the wooden storage box, wall-mounted utensil rack and clock with bold black numbers.

The look: This small kitchen was fitted from scratch using bargain units from a DIY store. In a layout that crams in as much storage as possible, with a full complement of wall cupboards as well as base units, their traditional detailing helps to add interest to the look of the room.

Color: The mellow wood of the units is complemented by matching strip flooring, dominating the room with glowing natural color. This is offset by the cooler tones of the splashback tiles, where blues and mauves in muted shades give the room a calming feel. A richer version of one of the mauves adds a further splash of color on the strip of wall above the units, while the white oven and pale countertops freshen the overall look.

Units: These wood-fronted units have traditional-style panelling and beading and metal handles. If you need to buy new units but have only a limited budget, take a look at the ranges available from DIY stores. The big-name superstores sell both flatpack and rigid furniture of reasonable quality at cheaper prices than most kitchen specialists. Some will expect you to arrange fitting and planning, while others offer a full service – make sure you get a quote before signing on the dotted line.

Floor: Hardwood strip flooring provides a warm, comfortable and practical surface for a kitchen. Cheaper veneers and laminate lookalikes are available, but for rooms with small floor areas even limited budgets may be able to run to the real thing, which is normally priced by the square meter.

KITCHEN TIP
To use space efficiently, look for a kitchen design that includes a selection of unit sizes. Even in a budget-priced range you should expect to find units in different widths, from 1 to 2ft – and with a choice of solid or glazed doors

The look: Glints of silver glam up this white kitchen. Metallic details embellish units and wall tiles, while the counter is lined with stainless steel appliances that shine so brightly you can see your face in them.

Color: In a color scheme designed to liven up the kitchen's existing fittings, touches of silver complement the pale grey of the counter as well as the clean whites of the units and wall tiles. The walls introduce brighter color in the form of a cool but spirit-lifting blue, while accessories add accents of warmer pink.

Units: White units are a versatile feature in a modern kitchen as they team well with many colors and styles of decor. If yours seem a little outdated, take a look at the handles – it's amazing what a difference a new set of knobs can make.

Sleek round ones give these existing doors a character change, while adding to the metallic elements in the room.

Splashback: The white wall tiles have also been tarted up with silvery detail – a border of triangles painted along the top edge of the splashback. Stick masking tape onto each tile to form the shape, then fill in with silver tile paint using an artist's brush. When dry, coat with clear tile varnish.

Accessories: Stainless steel appliances add high-tech glamour to the plainest kitchen, and this toaster and kettle have retro curves for added chic. A mini drawer unit makes a handy container for spices. Painted blue and pink, it reflects the colors of the glassware and vases on the sill.

The look: Amazingly, drab white and grey once pervaded this kitchen. Chic contemporary colors and materials now shine from every corner – and this smart scheme was pulled off without replacing a single unit.

Color: Lavender brings an air of modern sophistication to a room, and the high-tech highlights provided by metallic surfaces and appliances complement its cool character. Lemon yellow gives it a lift, and sharpens up the overall look, while pale grey flooring teams beautifully with both colors.

Units: The well-made but boring units have been licked into more stylish shape with a coat of melamine primer followed by lavender eggshell paint and acrylic varnish. The old granite-effect counter was not so easy to update, so has been replaced with a surface of chunky beech. Fitting a new countertop offered the opportunity to continue it across the end wall, providing additional work space. Sheets of stainless steel conceal the white splashback.

Shelves: Leftover pieces of worktop fixed to the side of the units make handy shelves for displaying good-looking gadgets and accessories. A tall free-standing shelf unit in the corridor takes care of kitchen overspill, including pots, pans and cook books.

Floor: Made from natural raw materials such as linseed oil, chalk, wood flour and pine resin, linoleum is a healthy, eco-friendly flooring. The smooth surface stops dirt from penetrating and discourages house dust mites. It is available in many colors and designs.

WHERE TO BUY:

UNITS

ALNO
Innovative designs featuring the latest colors and materials.
Tel: 617 482 2566
www.alno.com

BERCELI
Wide range of products for kitchen refinishing including cabinets and tempered glass sinks.
Tel: 877 9 berceli
www.berceli.com

CANYON CREEK CABINET COMPANY
Cabinets and islands built just for you. Choice of woods and custom design.
Tel: 228 0801
www.canyoncreek.com

CROWN POINT
Several styles including Shaker, Arts and Crafts, Milk Paint, and Victorian.
Tel: 800 000 4994
www.crown-point.com

HAAS CABINET CO., INC.
Custom cabinets for the entire home built to your specifications in a choice of woods.
Tel: 800 457 6458
www.haascabinets.com

IKEA
Value-for-money fitted and modular units in modern styles.
Tel: 516 681 4532
www.ikea-usa.com

KENNEBEC COMPANY
Period and handcrafted wood cabinets.
Tel: 207 443 2131
www.kennebeccompany.com

KITCHENCRAFT CABINETS
Different woods and designer selections of cabinet doors and kitchens. In Canada.
Tel: 800 463 9707
www.kitchencraft.com

KRAFTMADE
Built-to-order cabinets for every room in your home.
Tel: 888 562 7744
www.kraftmade.com

LOWES
Has everything you could need for a kitchen makeover.
Tel: 800 44 LOWES
www.lowes.com

MILLS PRIDE
Allows you to design your kitchen online.
Tel: 800 441 0337
www.millspride.com

STUDIO BECKER
Wodd cabinets for your entire home.
Tel: 510 865 1616
www.studiobecker.com

STYLECRAFT
Built-in and freestanding custom kitchens.
Tel: 717 445 6270
www.stylecraftcabinets.com

THOMASVILLE CABINETRY
Cabinetry for your entire household in a selection of collections.
Tel: 800 756 6497
www.thomasvillecabinetry.com

WOOD-MODE
Fine wood cabinets in a selection of designs, colors and styles.
www.wood-mode.com

AMEROCK
Wide selection of decorative and functional hinges and knobs, as well as storage solutions.
www.amerock.com

ATLAS HOMEWARES
Everything you could possibly need for a door.
www.atlashomewares.com

REPLACEMENT UNIT DOORS AND HANDLES

BAUERWARE
Wide selection of knobs including vintage, contemporary and games. Online catalog.
www.bauerware.com

CAPE COD BRASS
Brass knobs and knockers for all your doors.
Tel: 877 560 2818
www.capecodbrass.com

KNOBS 'N KNOCKERS
Decorative hardware for every room in your home.
Tel: 215 794 8045
www.knobsnknockers.com

LIBERTY HARDWARE
A selection of knobs and handles for all your doors and drawers.
www.libertyhardware.com

NEVERLAND KNOBS
Whimsical and colorful hand-painted wooden cabinet and furniture knobs.
Tel: 281 344 1720
www.neverlandknobs.com

APPLIANCES

AMANA
High-quality refrigerators and dishwashers, as well as other household appliances.
Tel: 800 628 5782
www.amana.com

ELMIRA STOVE WORKS
1950's retro stoves, refrigerators and other appliances.
Tel: 800 295 8498
www.elmirastoveworks.com

FRIGIDAIR
Refrigerators and freezers in
all shapes, styles sizes and
colors to fit your decor.
www.frigidair.com

GE
Appliances for your entire
household from a name
you know and trust.
Tel:800 626 2000
www.ge.com

GOOD TIME STOVE CO.
Antique stoves and ranges.
Tel: 01952 642000
www.goodtimestove.com

JC PENNEY
Retailers of most of the major
appliance brands.
Tel:800 222 6161
www.jcpenney.com

KITCHEN AID
Appliances large and small in
colors to go with every
kitchen.
Tel: 800 5412 6390
(countertop appliances)
888 222 8608
(major appliances)
www.kitchenaid.com

MAYTAG
High-quality appliances to
fit your every need.
Tel: 800 688 9900
www.maytag.com

MIELE
High-quality German-made
appliances with the latest
electronic features.
www.mieleusa.com

SEARS
Retailers of most of the major
appliance brands.
www.searshomecenter.com

SUB-ZERO
Built-in and integrated refrigerators of restaurant quality in
your home.
Tel: 800 222 7820
www.subzero.com

VIKING RANGES
Commercial-style ranges in
your own home.
Tel: 888 VIKING 1

WHIRLPOOL
Wide range of mid-market
built-in and freestanding
appliances.
Tel: 800 253 1301
www.whirlpool.com

SINKS AND TAPS

AMERICAN STANDARD
Sinks, faucets and accessories in a wide range of modern styles.
Tel: 800 442 1902
www.americanstandard-us.com

BATES AND BATES
A wide collection of sinks in metals, stone, ceramic and stainless steel.
Tel: 800 726 7680
www.batesandbates.com

BLANCO
Stylish German-made sinks, taps and waste disposal units.
www.blanco-america.com

DELTA FAUCETS
Well known purveyors of sinks and faucets with a design-your-own-faucet option.
www.deltafaucet.com

KOHLER
Wide range of sinks and faucets in the most popular styles.
www.kohler.com

KWC FAUCETS
Faucets and sinks to fit any decor.
Tel: 877 592 3287
www.kwcfaucets.com

MOEN
Designer-style sinks in stainless steel and other popular material with many collections to choose from.
Tel: 800 BUY MOEN
www.moen.com

PRICE PFISTER
Ceramic and stainless steel faucets and sinks.
Tel: 800 PFAUCET
www.pricepfister.com

STONE FOREST
Handcrafted granite sinks.
Tel: 888 682 2987
www.stoneforest.com

AVONITE
Countertops and sinks in various colors and styles.
Tel: 800 428 6648
www.avonite.com

CONCRETEWORKS
Concrete kitchen counters in several different shades.
Tel: 732 3909944
www.concreteworks.com

CORIAN
Kitchen and bath collections in a range of finishes.
Tel: 800 426 7426
www.corian.com

FOUNTAINHEAD
A wide selectionof collections in different colors and patterns.
Tel: 877 386 4323
www.ftnhead.com

HOME DEPOT
A selection of DIY and premade countertops.
Tel: 800 430 3376
www.homedepot.com

LOWES
A selection of DIY and premade countertops.
Tel: 800 44 LOWES

SILESTONE
Made of 93 percent quartz, these counters come in a variety of colors.
www.silestoneusa.com

SWANSTONE
Many collections in a variety of colors and patterns for the kitchen and bath.
Tel: 800 325 7008
www.swancorp.com

SPLASHBACKS

ANN SACK TILES
A wide range of tiles on many colors, styles and collections.
Tel: 800 278 8453
www.annsacktile.com

BROOKS
Stainless steel and copper splashbacks and counters, sinks and vents. Brass and wood also available.
Tel: 800 244 5432
www.brookswood.com

COLD SPRING GRANITE
Granite countertops for the kitchen and bathroom.
Tel: 320 685 3621
www.coldspringgranite.com

DECO ART TILE
A wide selection of colors and patters, with many different collections to fit any decor.
Tel: 800 331 8509
www.decoarttile.com

DECORATIVE CERAMIC TILE
A wide selection of handcrafted ceramic tiles and wood frame designs.
Tel: 630 924 5861
www.decorativeceramictile.com

FIREWORKS TILES
A variety of handpainted and handcrafted ceramic tiles for counters and splashbacks.
Tel: 540 675 9905
www.fireworktiles.com

FRIGO DESIGN
Copper and stainless steel, quilted patterns. Available in metal alloy.
Tel: 800 836 8746
www.frigodesign.com

TILE FANTASTIC
Ceramic clay bisque tile (red and white), glass and mosaic tiles Floor tiling also available.
Tel: 408 371 6247
www. tilefantastic.com

ACE HARDWARE

Paint and paint supplies including stencils and painting advice.
Tel: 630 990 6600
www.acehardware.com

BENJAMIN MOORE

A wide selection of indoor and outdoor paints and stains in many colors and finishes.
Tel: 800 344 0400
www.benjaminmoore.com

BIOSHIELD

Solvent free and water based house paint for a heathier household. Many colors and finishes available.
Tel: 800 621 2591
wwwecopaint.com

DUTCH BOY

Well-known for their interior and exterior paint, this company offers a wide variety of colors and finishes.
Tel: 800 828 5669
www.ducthboy.com

GLIDDEN

Well-known for their paint, this company offers a wide variety of colors and finishes.
Tel: 800 GLIDDEN
www.gliddenpaint.com

HOME DEPOT

Major retail outlet for all your home improvement needs, they carry many designer paint brands as well as lower priced ones.
Tel: 800 430 3376
www.homedepot.com

LOWES

Popular retail outlet for all your home improvement needs, they also carry paint brands.
Tel: 800 44 LOWES
www.lowes.com

FLOORING

ARMSTRONG
Linoleum and vinyl in a
selection of wood and stone,
smooth or textured.
Tel: 800 233 3823
www.armstrong.com

CARPET INNOVATIONS
Sisal, coirs, wool seagrass
and jute flooring.
Tel: 800 457 4457
www.carpetinnovations.com

CLASSEN
A large selection of wood
laminate flooring.
Tel: 800 834 8664
www.classenusa.com

CROSSVILLE CERAMIC
Porcelain and stone in a
variety of colors and designs.
Tel: 931 484 2110
www.crossville-ceramics.
com

DALSOCONGOLEUM
Wood, stone and tile
laminate and linoleum.
Tel: 800 274 3266
www.congoleum.com

E.Z. ORIENTAL INC.
Bamboo flooring in several
finishes.
Tel: 888 395 8887
www.bamboofloor.net

HEARTWOOD PINE FLOORS
Pine floors in a variety
of finishes.
Tel: 800 524 7463
www.heartwoodpine.com

JELINEK GROUP
Finished and nonfinished cork
floors in several colors, tree
and environment friendly.
Tel: 716 439 4644
www.corkstore.com

UNIVERSAL SLATE
Natural stone flooring in
slate and limestone as well
as mosaic tiles.
Tel: 888 677 5283
www.universalslate.com

ALTAMIRA LIGHTING
Unique metal and resin table and floor lamps with unique shades and finials.
Tel: 401 245 7676
www.aliamiralighting.com

BLOOMING LIGHTS
Unique lighting with hand-made metal mesh lampshades in copper, brass, and stainless, featuring flower shapes. All items are made-to-order.
Tel: 800 295 0559
www.bloominglights.com

CRATE AND BARREL
Huge range of light fixtures, from traditional to cutting-edge.
Tel: 800 967 6696
www.crateandbarrel.com

DESIGN WITHIN REACH
Contemporary desk, floor, and hanging lights.
Tel: 800 944 2233
www.dwr.com

IKEA
Affordable lighting, including track and spotlight systems.
Tel: 516 681 4532
www.ikea-usa.com

LIGHTING STORE USA
All kinds of lighting fixtures and contemporary lamps. Available online only.
www.lightingstoreusa.com

RUTH'S LAMPS AND SHADES, INC.
Custom made lampshades in a variety of styles and fabrics.
Tel: 215 836 1101
www.ruthslampsandshades.com

SHADES OF LIGHT
Table and floor lamps, ceiling fixtures, sconces, chandeliers, and more.
Tel: 800 262 6612
www.shades-of-light.com

VINTAGE LIGHTING
Rewired and restored fixtures of electric, converted gas and combination lighting.
Tel: 705 742 8078
www.vintagelighting.com

LIGHTING AND HEATING

WINDOW TREATMENTS

BED BATH AND BEYOND
Window hardware, curtain panels, sheers, and bed canopies.
Tel: 800 GO BEYOND
www.bedbathandbeyond.com

HUNTER DOUGLAS
Vertical and horizontal blinds in many styles, colors and materials.
Tel: 800 937 7895
www.hunterdouglas.com

KESTREL
Interior and exterior wooden shutters and blinds. Also carry wooden hurrican shutters.
Tel: 800 494 4321
www.diyshutters.com

LEVOLOR
A wide range of window shades, mini-blinds, vertical blinds and other window treatments in a wide range of materials.
www.levolor.com

NORTHERN BLINDS
Wood and faux wood blinds, roller curtains, woven shadings.
Tel: 877 861 5023
www.northernblinds.com

RESTORATION HARDWARE
Lighting solutions for every room and every decor.
Tel: 800 762 1005
www.restorationhardware.com

RUE DE FRANCE
Windor decor with a French country theme.
www.ruedefrance.com

SMITH AND NOBLE
Wood blinds, Durawood blinds, natural Roman shades and shutters and much more.
Tel: 800 560 0027
www.smithandnoble.com

SPIEGEL
Ready-made curtain panels, sheers and toppers, in some pretty designs.
Tel: 800 527 1577
www.spiegel.com

BED BATH AND BEYOND
Teapots, utensils, toasters
and more for the kitchen.
Tel: 800 GO BEYOND
www.bedbathandbeyond.com

BLOOMINGDALES
Toasters, coffe makers,
table linens, flatware,
dishes and more.
Tel: 800 472 0788
www.bloomingdales.com

BROOKSTONE
Upscale shelving, utensils and
stainless steel garbage cans.
Tel: 800 846 3000
www.brookstone.com

CRATE AND BARREL
Tableware, cookware and
flatware.
Tel: 800 967 6696
www.crateandbarrel.com

DEAN AND DELUCA
Kitchenwares and cookwares
as well as fine foods, infused
oils and other kitchen needs.
Tel: 877 826 9246
www.dean-deluca.com

GUMPS
Mail order trivets, fun
and fancy salt and pepper
shakers and mother of
pearl table accents.
Tel: 800 882 8055
www.gumpsbymail.com

IKEA
Smaller kitchen accessories,
storage, placemats and tables.
Tel: 516 681 4532
www.ikea-usa.com

KMART
Inexpensive source for
practical and stylish tableware,
cookware and small appli-
ances. Featuring the Martha
Stewart line of products.
Tel: 800 24 KMART
www.bluelight.com

MACYS
Toasters, coffe makers, table
linens, flatware,dishes and
more Infused oils and other
fine food items also available.
Tel: 800 BUY MACY
www.macys.com

NEIMAN MARCUS
Glassware, cookware, small
kitchen appliances. Cookie jars
and other fun canisters.
Tel: 888 888 4757
www.neimanmarcus.com

PIER ONE
Wine and spice racks, baskets
for storage, glass bottles,
ceramic canisters and
dishracks.
Tel: 800 245 4595
www.pier1.com

POTTERY BARN
Flatware and utensils,
tablelinens and cocktail
shakers.
Tel: 888 779 5176
www.potterybarn.com

SPIEGEL
Cookware, baking needs, small
appliances and tableware.
Tel: 800 527 1577
www.spiegel.com

WILLIAMS SONOMA
Dinnerware, small appliances,
teapots, cookware and cutlery.
Tel: 877 812 6235
www.williams-sonoma.com

UMBRA
Colorful placemats, fun and
functional dishracks.
Tel: 800 387 5122
www.umbra.com

ACE HARDWARE
Helpful advice for painting, installations, working with tools, lighting and toerh electrical equiptment.
Tel: 630 990 6600
www.acehardware.com

BENJAMIN MOORE
Helpful tips for painting and getting the decorative effects you want.
Tel: 800 344 0400
www.benjaminmoore.com

BETTER HOMES AND GARDENS
Advice on decorating and arranging all the rooms in the house from the magazine experts.
www.bhg.com

CONSUMER REPORTS
Reports on all major appliances and nearly all brand name products, including mattresses.
www.consumerreports.org

HOME DEPOT
Helpful tips fpr paintings, putting in bathroom fixtures and lighting and more.
Tel: 800 430 3376
www.homedepot.com

SEARS
The retailers of most of the major appliance brands are more than willing to give helpful advice on all of them.
www.searshomecenter.com

STENCIL ARTISANS LEAGUE, INC.
Helpful stencil tips, where to find the best designs and more.
Tel: 505 865 9119
www.sali.com

ADVICE